Teaching to ~~Learn~~

Learning to Teach

"Anne French Dalke's courageous investigation of her own teaching practice provides those of us who can't help questioning ourselves as teachers with the solace of companionship, the wisdom of experience, and an unexpected sense of our own dignity as pilgrims on the path."

Jane Tompkins, Author of A Life in School: What the Teacher Learned

"I'm moved and excited by this remarkable book. It will surely help all readers to be much braver and wiser in the pursuit of teaching that is both intellectually sophisticated and resolutely honest. I recommend it with great enthusiasm."

Peter Elbow, Author of Writing with Power; Embracing Contraries in Learning and Teaching; *and* Everyone Can Write

"*Teaching to Learn/Learning to Teach* is a feast, a book to savor and share. Beautifully written, it is deeply grounded in classroom experience. But the voices you hear in this book are not those of teachers alone. Students speak here as well, and they speak with insight and power, reminding us how pedagogical theory and practice both suffer when students are silenced. Listen to the voices in this compelling book and your sense of what it means to teach and learn will be transformed."

Parker J. Palmer, Author of The Courage to Teach *and* Let Your Life Speak

"The meditation is an ancient and supple form which Anne French Dalke retrieves to reflect upon her teaching life. I don't know anyone who has gone as far as she has in soliciting, receiving, and pondering her students' own words, incorporated here as a substantial part of the text. The tendency of women students to stand back particularly confounds us. Dalke ponders their withdrawal with recourse to current scholarship, to her own formidable experience as a Quaker teacher at a prestigious women's college, and to student texts that both challenge and honor the work we are trying to do together. One of the most important and original preoccupations of this book is Dalke's concern with a kind of hermeneutics of silence, a radical, generous, and scary move. 'Quaking we enter the classroom,' Dalke begins. Quaking, I leave this book, for it calls into question the foundations of my teaching life."

Mary Rose O'Reilley, Author of The Peaceable Classroom; Radical Presence: Teaching as Contemplative Practice; *and* The Barn at the End of the World

Teaching to Learn
Learning to Teach

STUDIES IN

EDUCATION & SPIRITUALITY

Peter L. Laurence and Victor H. Kazanjian, Jr.
General Editors

Vol. 4

PETER LANG
New York • Washington, D.C./Baltimore • Bern
Frankfurt am Main • Berlin • Brussels • Vienna • Oxford

Anne French Dalke

Teaching to Learn
Learning to Teach

Meditations on the Classroom

PETER LANG
New York • Washington, D.C./Baltimore • Bern
Frankfurt am Main • Berlin • Brussels • Vienna • Oxford

Library of Congress Cataloging-in-Publication Data

Dalke, Anne French.
Teaching to learn/learning to teach: meditations on the classroom / Anne French Dalke.
p. cm. — (Studies in education and spirituality; vol. 4)
Includes bibliographical references and index.
1. College teaching—Religious aspects. 2. Learning—Religious aspects.
3. Feminism and education. 4. Critical pedagogy.
5. Dalke, Anne French. I. Title. II. Series.
LB2331 .D347   378.1'25—dc21   2001038816
ISBN 0-8204-5753-1
ISSN 1527-8247

Die Deutsche Bibliothek-CIP-Einheitsaufnahme

Dalke, Anne French:
Teaching to learn/learning to teach: meditations on the classroom / Anne French Dalke.
−New York; Washington, D.C./Baltimore; Bern;
Frankfurt am Main; Berlin; Brussels; Vienna; Oxford: Lang.
(Studies in education and spirituality; Vol. 4)
ISBN 0-8204-5753-1

Cover design by Lisa Dillon
Cover art: *Classroom*. Taylor Hall, Bryn Mawr College.
Photograph by Carlos Garcia.

The paper in this book meets the guidelines for permanence and durability
of the Committee on Production Guidelines for Book Longevity
of the Council of Library Resources.

Printed in the United States of America

To Jeff,
who has kept me
company all along

I discovered in the thesaurus that teaching and learning are listed as antonyms of each other…[and] decided to invent a new word that combines them…:"tearning." Said out loud, it sounds like "turning"… and evokes our efforts to turn, shift and change the world.

Alisa Conner
Bryn Mawr student (1994)

Turning and turning in the widening gyre
The falcon cannot hear the falconer;
Things fall apart; the centre cannot hold…

William Butler Yeats
"The Second Coming" (1919)

To turn, turn will be our delight,
'Till by turning, turning we come 'round right.

"Simple Gifts"
American Shaker Tune

❋ Acknowledgments

I am grateful to all the students and colleagues whose musings are included here and on whose classroom practices I continually model and re-model my own.

I am grateful, too, to Bryn Mawr College, for employment (the occasion for writing this book); for a professional development leave in 1998–1999, during which I wrote most of this volume; and for a grant in Spring 2001 to help prepare it for publication. I am especially grateful to Alexa Antanavage who accomplished that work with such joyful goodwill and expertise, to Carlos Garcia for his photographs, and to Barbara Grubb for her generous archival assistance.

I also gratefully acknowledge permission to reprint my earlier work:

Chapter One was first published in *JGE: The Journal of General Education* 44, 3 (1995).

Chapter Two was first published in *Women's Studies: An Interdisciplinary Journal* 28 (1999).

Portions of Chapter Four were also published previously in other forms:

"Birthquakes/ Quaking Berths/ Crossroads/ Cross Purposes: Closing Address for the 17th Annual Lilly Conference on College Teaching, November 23, 1997" (with Linda-Susan Beard, Susan Dean and Jane Hedley). *Journal on Excellence in College Teaching* (1999).

"'On Behalf of the Standard of Silence': American Female Modernists and the Powers of Restraint." *Soundings:An Interdisciplinary Journal* 78, 3–4 (Fall-Winter 1995). 501–519.

❋ Table of Contents

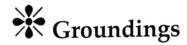 Groundings

Quaking, we enter the classroom. We take seats, cramped together around a big table. We sit there, waiting. Large windows surround us.

Or the room is more spacious, and we are seated further apart. In both classes, we form a circle, facing one another, but the expanse that separates us is huge.

Soon some of us will begin to speak—insistently, persistently, predictably; others will be more tentative, hesitant. Still others will find it impossible (or useless) to speak into, or across, that space.

The teacher enters the silence. She is at the apex. (Does a circle have an apex?)

She speaks first.

This book is a witness to the work I have been doing for the past twenty years of my life. A testimony to my teaching, it takes the form of multiple stories, written contrapuntally with myself, my students, and other teachers with whom I have been learning. Together we reconstruct the texts that have been our classrooms in the hope that others may find here useful accounts of the range of what may happen, both in the charged space that is the liberal arts classroom and in the spaces surrounding it. In telling these stories, I call attention in particular to some of the benefits of regular part-time arrangements for faculty, for students and for the more general outcomes of American education. I hope thereby to intervene in, and offer an alternative to, the by-now predictable lament about the overuse, and misuse, of part-time teachers.

I write out of and about a specific site, about specific sorts of teaching, learning, and "tearning" made possible by the interaction of individual professors and students in a specific location. I offer this project as one form of what Ursula Kelly calls an "ethnopedagogy," an account of what happens in the particular spaces we occupy (117), but also as a much larger en-visioning. I remember my experiences in the place Toni Morrison names paradise in order to imagine further the work I feel called to do, to sustain and extend that space.

I and my collaborators are situated both in the English Department (the location is actually called English House) and in an interstitial program called Feminist and Gender Studies at Bryn Mawr, a small private liberal arts college for women fifteen miles west of Philadelphia. Founded by Quakers in 1885, the college today is insistently secular. The courses offered in the English Department delight in texts: they are largely literary and print centered, but they also now often interrogate that focus and are increasingly interdisciplinary in conception. Prodded by co-teachers trained in other disciplines and postmodern devel-opments within our own, English professors are asking their students to consider why we should care so much about what these texts seem to say to us, about how they say it, about how we say what it is they say. The courses offered in the Gender Studies Program, which question gender roles, socialization, and bias, are even more varied, ambitious—sometimes confused and contradictory—in terms of objectives and methodology.

What attracted me to Bryn Mawr, and has in large part kept me here, are the interested and interesting colleagues I have to think-and-work with, people who care about what happens to each other both in the classroom and outside of it as well as about the difference that thinking carefully about ideas can make in our shaping of the world. The work we are able to do together in our classes is determined, in part, by where we come from, what we are reacting to, what we need and desire; it is limited but also enlarged—certainly each of us is often prodded beyond our limits—by the longings of others in the class, by the psychic and social scripts, conscious and unconscious, which each of us brings with us to Bryn Mawr. Our classroom work is further scripted by the college itself and by the larger premises informing North American higher education on which Bryn Mawr draws.

The college's mission statement does not acknowledge the complex force-field that we experience in our classes and that postmodern pedagogical theorists have recently explicated in such detail. The introduction to the 2000–2001 *Undergraduate College Catalogue*, for instance, is distinguished by its reiteration that the students here are "free":

> the College is...traditional in its commitment to the original medieval sense of the phrase "liberal arts." Then, as now, these were the studies of the free person—"free" not only to undertake such a broad education, without the necessity to specialize, but also free to question or advocate any idea without fear of reprisal. While both of these freedoms come from without, Bryn Mawr believes that such an education ultimately creates an even greater freedom within the individual. This is the freedom that comes from an education that leads one out of narrowness and prejudices of one's own experiences and toward a fuller awareness of oneself and the world.
>
> Bryn Mawr College is convinced that intellectual enrichment and discipline provide a sound foundation for living. It believes in the rights of the individual and regards the college community as a proving ground for the freedom of individuals to think and act as intelligent and responsible members of a democratic society. (24)

This opening statement of what "the college believes" is of course aimed at encouraging students to come here and is thus unlikely to call attention to the complications of the enterprise in which we are engaged. But such a vision of education as a rite—and right—of free individual development may be a source of much of the misfiring that occurs in our classrooms. The official introduction to the college acknowledges some of the opportunities but not the limitations of the psychic and social structures in which we are positioned. I attend here to both of these dimensions of our classroom interplay, trying for what Jennifer Gore calls "a greater acknowledgment of 'the order of things' we all inhabit…'a thick perception' of the present" (134).

In my description of Bryn Mawr classrooms I draw on but also acknowledge the contradictory presumptions of a broad range of experiences and critical perspectives including those of critical pedagogy, literary studies, gender studies, cultural studies, performance studies, and Quaker religious practice. I have been assisted by Gore's book, *The Struggle for Pedagogies: Critical and Feminist Discourses as Regimes of Truth*, which focuses on the difficulty of throwing off the regulative aspects of pedagogy. Other recent work that examines the psychic dimensions of the classroom, such as Sharon Todd's collection *Learning Desire* and Ursula Kelly's study, *Schooling Desire*, has also been quite helpful to me. Todd and Kelly are both mindful of the affective investments that are collected and exacerbated in the small social spaces that are my classrooms. Even more useful to me have been the explorations, like those of Laurie Finke, which both challenge the consideration of teaching as a conscious, rational, public practice and attempt to integrate psychoanalytic and political pedagogies (12). Roger Simon also examines the intersection of these dimensions of classroom work—the vested interests we bring to these spaces, and the larger social forces which structure our engagements there. I have found his consideration of the ways in which the "spillage of desire" disrupts the "process of inscription of the social order" especially helpful (8). Most important, however, has been the visionary work of bell hooks and of Quaker teachers like Paul Lacey, Mary Rose O'Reilley, and

Parker Palmer, who are open always to the expansive potential of the world in which we live and work.

Each of the chapters of this book also explores a specific metaphor for what happens in the classes in which I participate. Speaking metaphorically and examining the metaphors we employ is a way of illuminating both the limits and possibilities of our pedagogical practices as well as of the language we use to describe them. As George Lakoff and Mark Johnson have shown, metaphors both highlight and hide: systematically focusing on one aspect of a relationship between two terms keeps us from seeing other connections. All metaphoric structuring is thus partial, never equating two concepts but only articulating one in terms of another. Some part will always not fit; at some point, the metaphor cannot be extended (13). I attend in these pages to the limits of but also to the potential suggested by the metaphors I construct to describe what happens in my classrooms. I offer here stories of what teaching is, can be, might be, not only in this location and time—Bryn Mawr College at the turn from the twentieth to the twenty-first century—but in others which differ from it in all sorts of substantial ways.

My reflection occurs in seven stages, which take the form of seven chapters. Excerpts from a series of faculty interviews conducted by Emily Willis, one of my returning students, serve as introduction to the whole. Dissatisfied with my colleagues' description of our common work as the ever-on-going construction of stories, Lee is convinced that she needs to "think deeper" about these matters. Her conviction works as both pre- and postlude to what follows.

Chapter One takes the form of a journal charting a ten-year evolution in my approach to teaching. Initially enchanted by the fetish that was-and-is the text, I became increasingly mindful of students who were not particularly engaged by my literary explorations. Provoked by their silences, their resistances, puzzled by their dismissals of, or disinterest in, my performative readings, I slowly became aware that the dynamic of our coming together in the classroom itself constituted a text in the cultural studies sense of sensuous, contextual, conflicted practices. These classes began to present themselves to me as workbooks that needed attending to, in the way that I had attended only to printed texts in the past, as narratives which could be read, re-read, and eventually re-worked, re-written.

In the second chapter I attempt such a re-writing. As I became increasingly troubled by the laments and dissatisfactions of my students, I tried to script my classes, to control what happened, to make them work better by formatting them according to the principles of a particular dynamic that arose out of and spoke to my own political, social, and religious beliefs. I re-designed my classes on the model of the Quaker Meeting for Business, in which each member meets the responsibility of a common project of shared understanding by speaking up and so contributing to the learning of us all.

The following chapters face up to the difficulties of such a conception, recording my growing awareness, and that of my students, that my re-writing the text in accord with a particular script in which I am heavily invested will inevitably fall short, because the other actors in the play are—sometimes unknow-ingly—following scripts other than mine. Eventually I realized that the shared assumptions that guide a Quaker Meeting for Business are not those of a Bryn Mawr classroom.

In *Toward a Poor Curriculum*, William Pinar and Madeline Grumet observe that "what is missing is the study of the student's point of view from the student's point of view" (17). This volume attends to that gap: it involves multiple re-readings with my students of their reactions to the classes we took together. Chapter Three offers an extended discussion with a Haverford College student, Abby Reed, in which she and I examine together her anger at what did (not) happen in our junior-level seminar in gender studies. We conceptualize the class as a failed dinner party, at which some chose not to eat or rather could not figure out how to be fed, hungry as they were.

Chapter Four brings into this dynamic the contributions of my friend and co-teacher, Kaye Edwards, who has labored with me to create spaces in which students such as Abby might speak. With Kaye, I explore the complexities of silence, as a practice of keeping people out of conversations and as a fertile resource for understanding—an invitation both to share in the sufferings of

questions, you are in danger of coloring what you find or how you interpret what you find, or both. The era we're in now is very theoretically oriented, very model oriented. This is just another way of making sense, of organizing material. These models have created a situation where a notion of pattern is developed in advance of looking at the evidence; one can get carried away and begin to believe that one's story is the truth. Therefore, late twentieth-century speak is marked by constant qualification. We use the conditional and subjunctive in our writing and our speaking. Our self-consciousness is one of the things that will describe us.

The past comes to us in shards. We play with the shards we have. It's really just a matter of presentation. We have to recognize how much of the whole picture we're missing, and the fact that we are dealing with only a part, the part that is knowable to us, the part that has been discovered to date. We admit now that there is much more to learn and that there is so much that is unknowable. In the last twenty-five years, both students and general audiences have become more and more able to tolerate this. They even enjoy the problem approach with all its qualifications. Students just revel in the problems.

At a dig, one tries to be objective, to be technically oriented. The excavator has to make decisions as she goes. These ongoing judgments are subjective in a way even if they are based on expertise. One tries to be open to all the possibilities. Imagination will set in. The fun part is in putting together the story of what was, or might have been.

I see all of life as seeking. To me there aren't any real, hard facts, anywhere probably, but rather only interpretations. Archaeology fits my general approach to life. What is factualness? What is interpretation? These are fundamental questions about life.

With these issues very much in mind, I had interviewed Peter Beckman, the chair of the Physics Department at Bryn Mawr. Without any prompting from me, Beckman raised the issue of storytelling and placed it at the very center of the scientific enterprise:

A scientist invents stories that help him explain to other people his view of external reality. Aesthetic pleasure is the driving force, the dominant guiding force in all of science. Scientific investigation is driven by a belief that nature is understandable, that you can tell a simple story. The reason our stories are complicated is that we don't yet understand them well enough to tell them in a simple way. For a story to be accepted widely, two things have to happen: one, it has to be agreed by a large number of people that is elegant, that it's a pretty story, and it would be neat if nature behaved that way; and two, it has to be predictive. In addition, the story has to be proven not-wrong-yet for a long time before it's accepted. Einstein's General Theory of Relativity is just a gorgeous and beautiful story about how space and time work. It satisfies and it has predicted some of the weirdest things. An elegant story or model predicts things that you would have never thought of; it predicts surprises. We should be funding people who are thinking about the fundamental stories of nature from a purely aesthetic point of view.

Basic research is a kind of play, and we're not paying people to play. We need to pay more people to play with their ideas. The concept of the best story to date is a more useful concept than that of absolute Truth. There are only two kinds of models: those that are wrong, and those that are not wrong yet. Everything's provisional, everything's temporary, everything's replaceable. There are no final stories out there, on any front.

Paul Grobstein, a neurologist and developmental biologist particularly interested in the relation between brain function and behavior, is Eleanor A. Bliss Professor of Biology at Bryn Mawr College. Like Beckman, he believes in and argues for the provisional nature of storytelling in the sciences:

"Data" and "theory" are commonly used terms, promoted by a particular perspective on science: that science proceeds in a rational, objective, and—at every local point in time—defensible way, that it is a process of discovery of the existing and stable properties of an external reality. I like "observation" better, because it indicates the very real connectedness between science and what humans do all the time anyway. A theory is just one way of accounting for things. It's a short description of the pattern in observations. As far as I'm concerned, it's just a hypothesis. One uses it until one has evidence that it's no longer useful.

Science is not able to deal in truth with a capital "T." By its very structure, it is always a summary of observations, and summaries are inevitably and necessarily subject to change over a long period of time and/or a large range of observations.

Anomalous observations are put to the side. Science does not do anything with them unless a pattern can be discerned. Scientists, being human, have an investment in their summaries being right.

We have a scientific tradition, rooted in a larger social tradition of in-dividuality and competitiveness, that doesn't make any sense. Science is fundamentally a communal activity; it doesn't make any sense except as a communal activity.

I don't believe that a stable vision of external reality is achievable. Not knowing if external reality exists out there freed me up. As long as I thought there was a truth out there, the whole enterprise felt very meager. I was worried that somebody else was going to get there before me. Or I worried that somebody else knew the answer, and I didn't. Or I worried that I'd come up with an answer, and somebody else would have beaten me to it. This notion of the stable external truth is actually a pretty oppressive concept. When I finally realized there wasn't any such thing, my reaction was to feel pretty good about it. I have enjoyable work to do for the rest of my life.

I have found that the quality of thought here has become quite medieval. That is to say, no one aspires any more to the truth, each feeling that that is best left to the religious sphere. Instead, it is the most well-thought-out argument that carries the day. It all seems so cowardly to me somehow: everyone couching their conclusions in the conditional and the subjective as a form of self-protection while appearing to be courteous. Why is everyone so afraid of being wrong? Is there no one left with the heart of a lion? Has the ideal fallen so from being brave and trustworthy to being right? I believe it has, and because of the rapidity of being proven wrong, everyone seems to have fallen into hiding behind middle-management consciousness. Where has it gone, the ability to roar with laughter on being found wrong? This is hard to write. My topic is in many ways too close to my heart. My researches have led me to think long thoughts about the function of colleges as finishing schools. Whatever the Quaker beliefs that began Bryn Mawr, it now serves to acculturate women to the rigors of upper-middle-class corporate culture. I cannot tell you how I abhor that culture.

Now, all these people have been truly kind to me, giving their time and speaking their minds. How am I to repay that kindness: by calling them cowards? No, that appalls me.

I have to think deeper.

Hallway in Thomas. Bryn Mawr College.
Photograph by Carlos Garcia. 2001.

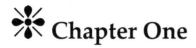 # Chapter One

A Journal of My Instruction:
Class as Text

For a number of years, Bryn Mawr offered a workshop for staff members who taught our required first-year course, Composition and Literature. At first, we brought in consultants to help us think about what we were doing: Kurt Spellmeyer, Gerald Graff, Peter Elbow visited and advised us. But later (when funds ran low), we decided to rely on our own good counsel. Several of us wrote papers describing what we were trying to do in our classes. My account takes the form of a ten-year history of the evolution of the course and of myself as its teacher, a chronicle of how I slowly came to see the class as a many-layered text which I could read, interpret and re-write.

May 1982: Looking for part-time work close to home, I go to interview in the English Department at Bryn Mawr. I've just earned my Ph.D. at the University of Pennsylvania; I've just delivered my second child. Ten days postpartum: no dress fits; my straps show; my milk is leaking. I've been teaching freshman English as a graduate student for the past four years but have no conscious pedagogy. (The workshops for teaching fellows didn't help much: we critiqued one another's assignments, graded one another's papers but talked very little about classroom dynamics.) I'm not prepared for the questions I get asked in this interview. I say that when I see the papers, I'll know what to do. I think I've blown it. They hire me anyway.

June 1982: The class I'll be offering follows the same format as the courses I've been teaching. Each first-year student is required to take a year-long course, Composition and Literature. She'll write multiple short papers in the first semester, longer ones in the second in response to a reading list that reflects her instructor's interests (I can design my own). I submit this syllabus, which I describe as "a course in the American novel." It reflects my understanding of what constitutes the best and most important fiction written in this country:

Poe, *Eighteen Best Stories*
Hawthorne, *The Scarlet Letter*
Melville, *Moby-Dick*
Clemens, *The Adventures of Huckleberry Finn*
Crane, *The Red Badge of Courage*
James, *The Portrait of a Lady*
Fitzgerald, *The Great Gatsby*
Hemingway, *The Sun Also Rises*
Faulkner, *The Sound and the Fury*
Bellow, *Seize the Day*

The director of the program calls: the syllabus looks fine, but (she asks delicately) how many of these texts will I do in the first semester? (I had planned, of course, to do them all.) Lesson #1: the students need time to read, to think, to write. Slow down. (Years later, I still will not have been able to put this lesson into practice.)

Fall 1982: I teach by distilling the lectures I heard in grad school, trying to encourage the students to respond to my readings of the texts, succeeding only fitfully. (I remember advice from my teaching supervisor at Penn: "never ask the class a question if you don't know the answer.") What I am offering, really, is an introduction to the study of English (well, American) literature. I imagine my audience as nineteen potential majors; I speak to them as if literature were as essential to their lives, and their making sense of their lives, as it is to me. But I know nothing about them, nothing about their desires, hopes, fears. They do tell me (I remember this as a group report) that they are drawn to this course because it "isn't women's studies." I remember, too, an enormous space between me, standing at the front of the room and lecturing, and them, clustered as close to the back wall as they can get, diligently taking notes. I like the note-taking; it makes me feel as though what I am telling them is worth their while. I'm teaching the same course at night at another women's college nearby. It's a pretty miserable experience: I get there late, harassed, and try to conduct a conversation with a group of tired, mostly older students, about texts they haven't read or haven't read well. I realize that this isn't the sort of teaching I want to do. I realize, too, that I want the class work to fit into a larger community of which I feel a part. I turn down the offer to teach there again in the spring.

Spring 1983: But I take on an extra course at Penn, an upper-level American literature course titled "The Fallen Woman." It's a version of the first-year course I'm teaching at Bryn Mawr (I add some texts to emphasize the theme: chunks of *Genesis* and *Paradise Lost* plus *Maggie, Sister Carrie, Lolita*). I get a chance to compare what goes on in (my) classrooms at the big school and the small one. At the big place, they're cockier, less intense, less engaged, just generally less interested. I decide that the smaller campus is really where I want to be.

But in April I accuse three of my first-year students of plagiarism. At the Honor Board hearing, I'm asked what I've done to cause this; something must be askew with my teaching. I'm furious at the allegation; can't they see how well I know the secondary material, how I'm posed to catch transgressions my colleagues don't even notice?

What strikes me now, however, is the combative, adversarial relationship that must have existed between me and my students. Here's part of one of my accusations:

> The charge of plagiarism against the student is set forth in the two accompanying documents. Her essay reproduces not only in substance but in choice of words the thesis of the article...I have underlined and marked in alphabetical notation the four paragraphs of the article which the student most clearly reproduces in her essay. Her paper is characterized not only by a lack of attribution, but the purloined passages form the fabric of her argument. Her borrowings, in other words, are not incidental but constitute the thesis of her paper.

Legalistic, overwritten, even alliterative—I am trying very hard here to summon the evidence, to fortify my position. Today, I'd handle this differently. I'd start with what the student knows about using sources. I'd show her how to use them more carefully. I'd try to help her, not accuse her. Eighteen years ago, then I think my job is to find 'em out, flush 'em out, expose 'em to the white light of truth, without giving them any clues about how to get there.

Well, I do give some clues. I take care to compare each new paper with the ones that precede it and ask each student to pass the ever-growing file of her work back and forth to me each week. I hope that when she opens the packet to enclose her most recent work, she'll review my comments from the week before.

My babysitter is Freyda Neyman, an undergraduate at Penn who expresses her surprise—her disappointment—that I'm teaching all canonical male authors. Her comment surprises me in turn. It's disconcerting to say so now, but nearly twenty years ago it really had not occurred (nor was it taught) to me that there were other texts in this tradition, other traditions in this literature. I slip *The Collected Stories of Katherine Anne Porter* into the end of the syllabus.

Summer 1983: I begin designing an entirely new, wholly female reading list for the fall, the distaff version of my first course. The summer's reading is exciting: wonderful new material, a wondrous introduction into my own history—as a woman and a mother—as I find it recorded in American literature. This is when my education begins: when I begin to educate myself.

Fall 1983: "Classic American Women Writers of the Nineteenth Century"
Chopin, *The Awakening*
Jewett, *The Country of the Pointed Firs and Other Stories*
Gilman, *The Yellow Wallpaper*
Spofford, "Circumstance"
Davis, *Life in the Iron Mills*
Dickinson, *Final Harvest*
Alcott, *Little Women*
Stowe, *Uncle Tom's Cabin*
I'm still offering a literature course: the traditional discipline, the traditional questions, seem to me to provide everything I and my students need. But now the works we are reading are about the lives of women. We begin—just a bit—to talk in class about the relation between these texts and our own lives. It's exhilarating for

me to teach this new material; my excitement spills over into writing, and I publish three articles—one on Dickinson, one on Spofford, one on Alcott. I begin to think that I've found my niche.

Spring 1984: I push on into the twentieth century, and into other forms, with drama, poetry and prose by the best-known and most respected contemporary American women writers.

Hellman, *Six Plays*
McCullers, *A Member of the Wedding*
Hansberry, *A Raisin in the Sun*
Bishop, *The Complete Poems*
Moore, *The Complete Poems*
Rich, *Poems Selected and New*
Sexton, *Complete Poems*
Walker, *The Color Purple*

The reading is lighter, more current, but these are genres I don't particularly favor, and the semester seems rather flat.

There is one illumination, however: I begin to realize that a group of articulate students who cluster on my right-hand side in the classroom are lesbians, that they are angry, and that their anger fuels the very pointed questions they have to ask about these texts. The morning after Adrienne Rich reads at a campus nearby, one of these students says (to those clustered on the left—and the gap that has opened up between the two groups is suddenly made visible to me): "*You* all should have come."

It occurs to me to ask the students for their suggestions for my next reading list. I'm embarrassed; I haven't heard of Audre Lorde, and misspell her name as I write it on the board.

My surprised discovery, in January 1984, that I'm pregnant again gives a particular point to earlier class discussions about choice and free will, about childbearing and childrearing in *The Awakening*. (At least I hope and think it does, and I tell my students so.) The chairman of the department offers me the option of "taking off a week or two." I realize that I can't deliver in September and still teach; I need the whole semester. Because this is a two-semester course, that means the whole year off.

September 27, 1984: The midwife sits on one side of the double bed, Jeff on the other. I push three times and cough once; our son Sam is born—that easily. I spend the night in bed with him, dozing, waking to marvel at his perfect self. The next morning the midwife brings me a loaf of the bread she was baking when called to assist at this birth.

Fall 1984: But it's a miserable year, first time in my life I haven't been working. I find a sitter for the mornings, go to the library and try to shape my dissertation into a book. A sorry business. It's not good enough to go as it is, but it would take more effort, more interest than I have now to re-do it. I begin to realize how much I need to be in conversation with others in order to work and think and write. I'm longing to be back in the classroom.

Spring 1985: Impelled by a vague desire to put our religious lives in order, looking for a community to support what we're teaching our kids, Jeff and I begin to attend Quaker Meeting. I'm in the midst of my second great awakening (the first was feminism, summer—fall 1973). It took a long time for my feminist consciousness (even a syllabus of women writers!) to filter into my classroom, but I am able to put my Quaker leadings into practice more quickly. I embark, first in worship, then at home and at school on the discipline of learning to listen. I realize that, as I learn to be a Quaker and a mother—as I learn, especially, to be attentive to my children—I am learning also to be a better teacher to my students.

With great excitement, I put together a new syllabus for the fall. Still extending my knowledge of American women authors, I'm aiming now for a collection of substantial fictional texts written in the first half of this century.

Fall 1985:
"Classic American Women Writers of the Twentieth Century"
Stein, *Three Lives*
Wharton, *Ghosts*
Glasgow, *Barren Ground*
Cather, *Death Comes for the Archbishop*
Hurston, *Their Eyes Were Watching Cod*
Welty, *Delta Wedding*
O'Connor, *The Violent Bear It Away*

I'm back with the sort of texts I love: big, thick ones. I'm increasingly conscious of what the students bring to the course, of the roles they can play in helping me decide what and how to teach. I offer the reading list to them as a course in process: which of these texts ought to be taught? (They reject *Barren Ground*—on the grounds that it's creaky, overwritten, melodramatic.)

Spring 1986: As in the last course, I supplement the novels with more contemporary work by American women in other genres—drama, poetry, and nonfiction.

Ozick, *Art and Ardor: Essays*
Moore, *The New Women's Theatre: Ten Plays*
Brooks, *Selected Poems*
Kumin, *Up Country*
Rukeyser, *The Collected Poems*
Levertov, *Poems 1960 to 1967*
Silko, *Ceremony*
Giovanni, *Gemini*

We start off well with Ozick's "Hole/Birth Catalogue" and "Justice to Feminism": she brings into the classroom questions we'll return to throughout the semester. In spite of (because of?) the students' resistance to thinking about themselves as women, in spite of (because of?) their resistance to studying at a women's college, I begin to conceive of the classroom as a community of women learning together. I experiment with concrete ways to make that work. I ask students to lead class discussion. They do it very poorly. I try to figure out how to help them do it better. I settle finally on this system (which I still use, because it works so well): several students are assigned to discuss the text ahead of time. Together they write up a paragraph (or page) of "real questions" they would like the class to try to answer. They set the agenda, but I guide the discussion, deciding where to linger, when to move forward.

The most articulate student, who has shown little patience with others during the year (she interrupts and overrides them often), asks me if she can knit in class. I don't mind (I knit myself in department meetings), but her classmates object vociferously. They see her knitting as an insult: it tells them that they aren't worth listening to, that their conversation is not important enough to engage her full attention. They tell her, angrily, how they've felt about her treatment of them all year. She insists that to respond quickly to their statements, even to interrupt, is her way of showing excitement about their ideas, that it's not disrespectful.

This is not an easy discussion to manage. I'm unaware of it yet, but we are beginning to construct a feminist pedagogy. The students begin objecting to my choice of texts, to my decision to give an exam. Inviting them to help decide about the conditions in which they learn opens me to challenges I'm not sure how to handle. But the classroom begins to seem a livelier place.

Just as I'm getting into it, my (thrice-renewed) year-long appointment ends. I was expecting this, but still I fall apart. I start therapy; it takes almost two years of work to figure out that I am doing with my life exactly what I want to be doing: reading, teaching, writing, raising kids. If trying to juggle those interests means the insecurity of part-time work, so be it.

Fall 1985—Spring 1986: I teach for a year—Major British Writers and Advanced Expository Writing—at Penn. It's hilarious to be back here, where I got my degree. My (former) professors pass me in the hall; do I look vaguely familiar to them? I enjoy my course although the students seem surprised at how much I ask them to do. But the evaluations show that they appreciate my interest in using their concerns to help shape their classes. They also see that I am learning along with them:

> "She structures the class to suit each individual student's needs"; "Willing to get to know her class. The class was very open"; "Willing to give extra time to students. Easily accessible"; "She is receptive to students' comments and suggestions"; "She didn't have total set mind on the reading, so she obviously worked very hard to learn and ignite some discussion"; "Although she told us in the beginning that she was not an expert in this subject, she never hesitated to research what she did not know."

Mixed in with the comments that I preen myself over, however, are a few that make me weep: "Students' opinions were dull, dull, dull, dull, dull," says one. I get, too, one clear repudiation of all I am trying to do (I find myself shaking, rereading it now):

> I was *incredibly* displeased with this class...As Anne is a mother as well as a junior faculty member, I can understand her commitments. However, my parents are paying too much money, and I am investing too much time, to have to take courses from a Professor who comes to class so poorly prepared. It is obvious that throughout the year she prepared for the class haphazardly at best, and instead relied on general class discussion, instead of on at least some (a minute amount) of prepared material. I am incredibly, totally displeased and annoyed...the class leadership was uninspired at best...

The charge of not being prepared upsets me the most. When the student comes to pick up his papers (including a reading journal filled with similar views), I burst into tears. I want to sit him down and explain how very hard I *have* prepared for each class, how much time I *have* spent trying to create an environment in which the students can work together to an understanding of the material that makes sense to them rather than simply being fed the opinions of "those who know." I want to tell him how wrong he is to want the sort of education I'm no longer willing to offer.

Now I wonder: was he?

Fall 1987: Pregnant for the fourth (last) time, I'm back at Bryn Mawr for another three-year stretch (and, thankfully, will get stretched again and again). The course I design for this round is consciously integrated, consciously dualistic (with the intention of dissolving dualisms): I pair each female writer with a complementary (contradictory?) male writer, and I begin to focus on issues of religion and spirituality (Quakerism is asserting itself).
"The Flesh and the Spirit"
Poe, *The Fall of Usher and Other Tales*
Gilman, *The Yellow Wallpaper*
Hawthorne, *The Scarlet Letter*
Jackson, *The Gifts of Power*
Douglass, *Narrative*
Dickinson, *Final Harvest*
Whitman, *Leaves of Grass*
Stowe, *Uncle Tom's Cabin*
Melville, *Moby-Dick*

Spring 1988: I continue the same pattern. But I also begin (finally, belatedly; I seem always to come to these realizations late)

to think about diversifying the American curriculum in terms of race and culture as well as gender:
Wharton, *Ghosts*
James, *The Turn of the Screw*
Chesnutt, *The Conjure Woman*
Twain, *The Adventures of Huckleberry Finn*
Alcott, *Little Women*
Zitkala-Sa, *American Indian Stories*
Neihardt, *Black Elk Speaks*
Pinzer, *The Maimie Papers*
Crane, *Maggie*

In staff workshops, we talk about making our classes more interdisciplinary, recognizing that most of our students won't be English majors, that many of them have little interest in traditional literary texts, that our discipline is opening up in ways that might interest them. These workshops also introduce me to the concept of "speculative instruments," which I find compelling, as a way of giving students a "hook," a handle for talking about texts. So in this course I promise we'll explore "political, social, economic" issues as well as "aesthetic" ones. For the first time, I require some "nonliterary" reading: an essay by Levine on slavery, and essays by Heilbrun, Rosaldo, and Saiving on female culture. I say to the students, you like *Huckleberry Finn*, but can't think of anything to write about? Then imagine what Levine might do with the text. Imagine a conversation between him and Mark Twain...

This room is smaller than those I've taught in before, the seating circular (though I perch on the table above the students), and I'm feeling very much at home, talking about issues that are not merely academic—for me or them. One day, when kindergarten is closed, I bring my daughter Lily with me to class; I ask her to sit quietly and color, but halfway through she gets up to mimic me: she writes on the board. The chalk screeches; I ask her to stop; she won't. This in the middle of a discussion of *Little Women*, of women's traditional roles, of the care of children, of the handling of anger. I am sharply conscious of the text and my life in juxtaposition, as possible models for the lives of my students. I decide to talk about how hard it is for me, some days, to get here.

I begin to see how being a good reader and writer connects with being a good citizen. In discussing these texts, I realize, I am teaching my students not only attentive reading and careful, clear writing but a kind of thoughtfulness they can use to guide their lives. Helping them become conscious of what they see when they read, of what they do when they write, will make them more aware of the ways in which the world has been constructed for them, of the ways in which they can reconstruct it for themselves. This is heady stuff; the classroom begins to seem larger and larger.

Fall 1988: My colleague Susan Dean recommends Paul Lauter's work to me; I use *Reconstructing American Literature* to draw up a course which is even more consciously political than the last one. I say that "we will listen together to voices which speak of the diversity of American literatures," that we will explore "the myth of the American Dream and its undersides as seen from a variety of cultural perspectives." I begin the course with a series of long-acknowledged texts and then slowly begin to introduce more newly uncovered "ethnic" work.
"American Dreams, American Nightmares"
Melville, "Bartleby," "Paradise...," "Benito Cereno"
Hawthorne, *The Scarlet Letter*
Faulkner, *Go Down, Moses*
Chesnutt, *The Conjure Woman*
Hurston, *Their Eyes Were Watching God*
Walker, *The Color Purple*
Fitzgerald, *The Great Gatsby*
Hemingway, *The Sun Also Rises*
Cather, *Death Comes for the Archbishop*
Pinzer, *The Maimie Papers*

Spring 1989: The balance tips the other way. I start with just one canonical text; the rest is a conscious attempt to give space to a variety of voices.
Crane, *Maggie*
Yezierska, *Bread Givers*
Kingston, *The Woman Warrior*
Silko, *Ceremony*
Anaya, *Bless Me, Ultima*
Paley, *Enormous Changes at the Last Minute*

Morrison, *Beloved*
poetry by Bishop, Brooks, Rich
Ozick on Yiddish, Wolf on Chinese, Allen on Native American, Levine on African American culture

We entertain a series of visitors from *McNeil/Lehrer News Hour* who are interested in our focus on ethnic diversity. The chance to promote my sort of teaching on national television tells me that what I'm doing in my classroom is of interest and value in the outside world. I'm a little nervous, though, about going public with my experiments.

I'm safe: we don't make the final cut.

One of the students is unhappy with the syllabus: she feels as if European American culture is being devalued in all the texts we read, white and other. I think she may be right: there's certainly no celebration of family life in Melville, Hawthorne, Faulkner, Hemingway, Fitzgerald. Their protagonists make their (unhappy) lives by repudiating others and going off alone. But characters in the other works, from other ethnic backgrounds, seem to find sanity and maturity by going home again, by instructing themselves (and us) in communal life. (Houston Baker develops this idea in *Long Black Song* and elsewhere.) I try to entice the student into exploring views other than those she feels she already knows and values, but I'm not successful. She transfers to a bigger co-ed school, where she hopes to feel more comfortable.

Prodded by faculty workshops on diversity in the college community, I think harder about the difficulty of constructing a class that recognizes differences both in the texts and in my students. I try to design a course that doesn't pit white against other, a course that defines American as ethnic. My colleague Diane Elam points out that in offering one Chicano, one Asian American, one Native American, one African American, one Jewish American text, I have replaced the melting pot theory with a series of stereotypes. I'll try, this time 'round, to cover fewer groups and so give more play to the complexity of each culture. I begin with a collection of Jewish, female European American, and African American works.

Fall 1989: "In Search of Community"
The Book of Ruth

Yezierska, *Bread Givers*
Tyler, *Dinner at the Homesick Restaurant*
Welty, *Delta Wedding*
Alcott, *Little Women*
Stowe, *Uncle Tom's Cabin*
Brent, *Incidents in the Life of a Slave Girl*
essays on Judaism by Ozick, Rosenfeld; on feminism by Rosaldo, Benhabib; on slave culture by Levine

Spring 1990: I start with an African American novel and then move on through groupings of Native American, Asian American, and Latino texts. By offering a variety of voices from each culture (Chin bickering with Kingston, Rivera with Rodriguez), I make it harder for my students to identify a single "group" voice.

Morrison, *Beloved*
Ruddick, "Maternal Thinking"
Levine, "The Fate of the Sacred World"
Silko, *Ceremony*
"The Origin Myth of Acoma," "The Winnebago Trickster Cycle," "The Walam Olum of the Delawares,"
Allen's "The Sacred Hoop"
Kingston, *The Woman Warrior*
Chin, *The Chickencoop Chinaman* and
"The Most Popular Book in China"
Rich, "Compulsory Heterosexuality" and "Twenty-One Love Poems"
Grahn, *Another Mother Tongue* and *The Work of A Common Woman*
Audre Lorde, *A Burst of Light* and *Chosen Poems*
Rodriguez, *Hunger of Memory*
Rivera, *...ye no se lo trago la tierra*

I tell the students, straight up, first class, that I have moral and political reasons for asking them to read these texts. I've chosen books that give me pleasure (and that I hope they'll enjoy reading). But I also have a very specific two-part agenda: I want us to learn about different cultures, and then I want us to think about constructing a community that acknowledges those differences. If ethnicity describes membership in a group that shares biology, language, traditions, memories, can we think together about how to construct another community, not of descent but of consent? (Sollors 4–5). Can we learn to see these tests not as an assault on our own cultural identity but rather as a celebration of options? I ask the students to write about an experience they've had of being in a community or an experience of being left out of one, to describe their initial reaction to the differences they've encountered so far on campus, to respond to my proposal for the course.

There are moments during the year when I am disheartened: I feel the students' resistance to different points of view; I see how threatened they feel by different constructions of the world. In a faculty discussion group, I come across another challenge to my evolving pedagogy. We read Iris Marion Young's critique of the ideal of community which, she argues,

> privileges unity over difference, immediacy over mediation, sympathy over recognition of the limits of one's understanding of others from their points of view. Community is an understandable dream...but politically problematic...because those motivated by it will tend to suppress differences among themselves or implicitly to exclude from their political groups persons with whom they do not identify...the desire for mutual identification in social relations generates exclusions...A desire for community...helps reproduce homogeneity... we need to attend to the irreducibility of difference. (1990, 300–301, 305)

Young offers an alternative, "a politics of difference...an openness to unassimilated otherness" (319). I find her argument convincing; I wonder if my project is altogether wrong-headed.

Yet by the end of second semester I'm feeling as though the course has worked after all. In several experimental presentations, the students ask us to view the world from perspectives other than our own: when we discuss Brent's book, for instance, the presenters ask us to read it as though we were slave owners. One thoughtful student prods our questioning: she thinks we exact higher standards of community from white groups than from those whites call "other." Another student hosts an end-of-the-year supper in her apartment, the first time that's happened. It feels as though the class itself has become a community. Several of the students say how important the work we've done together seems to them; one of them suggests that this course be required for all first-year students, a substitute for the diversity seminar that is offered during orientation. The process takes time, they agree, but is crucial if a diversified college is to flourish as a community.

On one count, though, I'm sure the course has not been successful (will I ever get it right?). Near the end of the second semester I've asked the students to read a group of writings by lesbians. I'm trying to add their perspectives on sexual orientation to the differences in gender, race, culture, class, and religion highlighted elsewhere in the course. But we don't have enough time to really work through the material; I end that portion of the class thinking that all I've accomplished is the confirmation of old prejudices.

This year and last I've been hearing complaints from my students about the visible lesbian community on campus. One student, who asks me to write a letter of recommendation to transfer, tells me how much it upsets her to see same-sex necking in the campus center. Another student says, "I'm not homophobic. But I do have questions." Convinced that sexual orientation is an important issue dividing members of this campus community from one another, I decide to spend next year's class focusing on that one topic. I'm sly. I write up a course description about "women's relationships." I plan to look, in the first semester, at texts about mothers and daughters. After fourteen "safe" weeks, we'll move into trickier territory.

Fall 1990: "Images of the Mother"
Brooks, "the mother," "The Womanhood"
Gilligan, "Concepts of Self and Morality"
Plath, "You're," "Morning Song," "Child"
Olds, "Exclusive," "For My Daughter," "35/10," "The Green Shirt," "Life with Sick Kids," "That Moment," "Looking at Them Asleep"
French, *Beyond Power*
Olsen, "Silences in Literature" and "I Stand Here Ironing"
Walker, "One Child of One's Own," "Beauty"
Paley, "Two Short Sad Stories"
Ruddick, "Maternal Thinking"
Paley, "Faith in the Afternoon" and "Faith in a Tree"

Ruddick, "Preservative Love"
Robinson, *Housekeeping*
Chodorow, "Family Structure and Feminine Personality"
Tyler, *Dinner at the Homesick Restaurant*
Smith, "Parenting and Property"
Kincaid, *Annie John*
Lugones, "Playfulness, 'World'-Traveling and Loving Perception"
Gordon, *Men and Angels*
Morrison, *Beloved*
Kingston, *The Woman Warrior*
Chernin, *In My Mother's House*

On the first day, I set up the general premises of the course, most of them gleaned from an essay about teaching writing, which my colleagues Jane Hedley and JoEllen Parker have just published and presented at a staff workshop. The particular application, though, is mine:

—Writing is a function of inquiry.

—The intellectual process engaged in the class is transferable to all other college work (and to life outside the classroom).

—The written work I'm asking for is a form of puzzle solving. In each essay, I'll ask you to recognize a problem, to investigate it, and to express the insight you've achieved by doing so.

—One particular puzzle will engage us this semester, that of the mother-daughter relation. What has been its history, in our own lives, in this country, in this century? What have been its tensions, its difficulties, its modes of resolution, in theory and in literature?

—The assignments are carefully sequenced. We'll begin with a series of inventories, in which I'll ask you simply to describe the texts you're reading, to write one-paragraph summaries of the arguments of the assigned essays. You are not to evaluate, not to respond but just to report the major points. Your second task will be to investigate a puzzle, that of your own mothers' lives, in the form of an autobiography. The third is to locate a gap, a problem, an issue that arises when you juxtapose two texts. Perhaps imagining, in preparation, a conversation between Ruddick and Paley (for instance)—first describing Ruddick's argument in a precis, then applying it to Paley's short story—is a useful way to begin this task.

—We'll start and end the semester with autobiographical assignments: the first a story of your own mother, the last imagining yourself as a mother (or choosing not to become one). I want, thus, to connect our academic work to our personal lives (but, frankly, I'm also trying to control students' insistent speaking about what they know experientially, trying to contain it at the semester's beginning and end, in hopes that it won't dominate all the discussions of the texts in between.)

So far, so good. But then I give a preview of next semester's work, which will look at women as friends and lovers—not of men, but of each other. I say that most of the writers in the second semester are lesbians and that I hope studying lesbianism in their texts will prove a means for both straight and gay students to understand some of the roles lesbians play on this campus. I tell them I hope that our classroom can be a safe place to explore these issues. After the first class, several young women go to JoEllen, who directs the first-year writing program, and complain about being bamboozled. She suggests they hang on.

Spring 1991: "Mothers and Lovers"
Rich, "Compulsory Heterosexuality"
Smith-Rosenberg, "The Female World of Love and Ritual"
Jewett, "Martha's Lady" and *The Country of the Pointed Firs*
O'Brien, "'The Thing Not Named': Willa Cather as a Lesbian Writer"
Cather, "On the Gulls' Road" and *My Antonia*
Stein, "Lifting Belly" and *Three Lives*
Sarton, *Plant Dreaming Deep*
Hoagland, *Lesbian Ethics*
Anzaldua, *Borderlands/La Frontera*
Rich, "The Eye of the Outsider"
Bishop, "First Death," "Filling Station," "In the Waiting Room," "One Art"
Lorde, "Uses of the Erotic"
Heywood, "Lesbianism and Feminist Theology"
Broumas, *Beginning with O*
Rich, "Twenty-One Love Poems"
Morrison, *Sula*
Walker, *The Color Purple*

Finally, finally, I've got it (almost) right. At the end of the year, the students who were resistant at the beginning are raving about how much they learned; the lesbians offer suggestions for additional reading. All of them insist that "everybody should take the class." I'm going to repeat it. Finally, I'm going to teach a course that isn't brand new. I'll have time to write.

June 1991: Susan Dean calls to tell me that the incoming class of nontraditional students ("older women") has doubled this year. A second section of Composition and Literature is being added for them; would I like to teach it? And use the syllabus she's been developing over the years for that population of students? So much for the easy prep. But I'm excited about the opportunity to work with students like myself, who are trying to balance work, school, and family commitments. I finally come out as a mother on campus; I ask to be assigned classrooms close to my office, so I can manage better on the days when I have sick kids in tow.

I settle down to read the syllabus, which takes my breath away: this is much more interdisciplinary, much broader in scope, than anything I've yet dared to tackle. The texts are more various, the questions they raise much larger than any I've dealt with so far. I'm being nudged further, and my students will be nudged with me beyond the attentive reading of "literary" texts.

Fall 1991: "Subjectivity/Objectivity"
Belenky, "Connected Teaching"
Keyes, "Flowers for Algernon"
Gogol, "Diary of a Madman"
Jackson, "The Lottery"
Mansfield, "The Lady's Maid"
Rich, "My Sister's Marriage"
De Maupassant, "Mademoiselle Pearl"
Porter, "Maria Concepcion"
Fuentes, "If We Had Left at Daybreak…"
Baldwin, "My Dungeon Shook: Letter to My Nephew"
Bennett, "The Birth of Jim Crow"
Woolf, "Mary Wollstonecraft"
Gallagher, "…Ursula LeGuin"
Horney, "The Dread of Woman"
Eliade, "Myth"
Woodham-Smith, *The Reason Why*
Carr, Chapter 1, *What Is History*

Geertz, Chapter 1, *The Interpretation of Culture*
Kuhn, *The Structure of Scientific Revolutions*
LeGuin, *The Left Hand of Darkness*
Scholes, "The Left Hand of Difference"
LeGuin, "Is Gender Necessary?"
Ozick, "Metaphor and Memory"
Dickens, *Great Expectations*

It's wonderful to read Belenky and company again, to be reintroduced to their version of Freire's liberatory pedagogy. I find this model of teaching absolutely compelling this time 'round and hope I'll be able to put it into practice with this new group of students:

> students need opportunities to watch...professors solve (and fail to solve) problems...They need models of thinking as a human, imperfect, and attainable activity...In Freire's "problem-posing" method, the object of knowledge is not the private property of the teacher. Rather, it is "a medium evoking the critical reflection of both teacher and students." Instead of the teacher thinking about the object privately and talking about it publically so that the students may store it, both teacher and students engage in the process of thinking, and they talk out what they are thinking in a public dialogue. (217, 219)

What a vision—and what a relief! It seems so freeing and so honest not to pretend that I have the answers to all questions which might present themselves in class. We'll all work together toward whatever answers might emerge.

Susan Dean doesn't tell me much about what she's after in this course; she invites me to make my own connections. (I realize she's practicing "connected teaching" on me, though what I want right now is the banking method.)

I describe the course to the students as a more ambitious project than a traditional composition and literature class: it's a general introduction to college-level critical thinking, to the particular kinds of thinking cultivated in the variety of disciplines offered for study here. It begins with texts that raise questions about point of view, about the reliability of the narrator. It moves on through discussions of how the disciplines of history, anthropology, science, and literary theory construct knowledge. It asks throughout what it means to think, what it means to think objectively, subjectively. How do people—women—you—learn? How can education be made accessible to those who haven't found it so? I invite the students to look at how they are taught, at the unspoken assumptions that guide their education and at the habits of thought it encourages. What, I ask, are the ends of education? What its most effective means? (With questions like these, it's no wonder I'm going to get into trouble before the year is out.)

Whew! On the first day of class, the excitement is palpable. I'm wondering if I can control and channel all this energy, all this intensity, during the course of the year. Jane Tompkins's "Pedagogy of the Distressed" (which one of the students, a friend of hers, passes on to me) describes exactly what working with these older students is like:

> every student in every class one "teaches" is a live volcano…I can never fool myself into believing that what I have to say is ultimately more important to the students than what they think and feel. I know now that each student is a walking field of energy teeming with agendas. Knowing this I can conduct my classes so as to tap into that energy field and elicit some of the agendas. (659)

I distribute copies of Tompkins's article to anyone who will listen to her (my) vision of what teaching can be:

> I've come to realize that the classroom…is the chance we have to practice whatever ideals we may cherish…And I wonder…if performing [our] competence in front of other people is all that that amounts to in the end…the main point for me was for the students, as the result of [the] course, to feel some deeper connection between what they were working on in class and who they were, the real concerns of their lives…I went from teaching as performance to teaching as a maternal or coaching activity because I wanted to remove myself from center stage and get out of the students' way, to pay more attention to them and less to myself…I made the move in order to democratize the classroom. (656, 658, 660)

Paying careful attention to these students means that I am convinced, by year's end, that no one should go to college before she's thirty, maybe forty. For the first time, it feels right to sit down at the table with my students, who write paper proposals like this one by Mary Wright:

> I am worried that I won't be able to fill twelve pages with either good ideas or good writing…My goal for this paper is for my discussion…to be full and rich and unhurried. I will be wary of distraction by detail. I will not be pretentious but will write clearly and simply. I will enjoy the journey.

And what a journey it is! These women are so certain that this work is important, so hungry to learn that they can't help but be fed. But feeding them is exhausting work. Some of them bring histories of failure or of abuse; others have learning disabilities (perhaps?) that create real obstacles to their writing papers. Others come with poor academic preparation; they need extra conferences, the option of doing re-writes. And they are demanding consumers.

I find out just how demanding during the second semester, when Susan Dean, who designed the course, is on leave. The dean of the college, Karen Tidmarsh, and I are using her syllabus. The course expresses a humanist's love affair with the social sciences, an Americanist's excitement about the evolving multicultural curriculum, one which invites the heretofore silent voices to speak. It focuses on questions of colonialism, class, and gender. It has worked well and repeatedly for Susan in the past. But Karen and I have a very hard time of it.

Spring 1992:
Shakespeare, *The Tempest*
Montaigne, "Of Cannibals"
Fiedler, "The World Without a West"
Hegel, "Lordship and Bondage"
Retamar, "Caliban"
Lamming, "The Occasion for Speaking"
Smitherman, "Where It's At"
LeGuin, "Bryn Mawr Commencement Address"
Rodriguez, *Hunger of Memory*
Smedley, *Daughter of Earth*
Gilligan, "Woman's Place in Man's Life Cycle"
Chodorow, "Family Structure and Feminine Personality"

Christ, Introduction, *Womanspirit Rising*
Keller, "Feminism and Science"
Schneider, "Our Failures Only Marry"
Rich, "Taking Women Students Seriously"
Mead, excerpts from *Mind, Self and Society*
Emerson, "Self-Reliance"
Fuller, "Woman in the Nineteenth Century"
Cobb and Sennett, *The Hidden Injuries of Class*
Berger, *Ways of Seeing*
Freire, *The Pedagogy of the Oppressed*

February 1992: Other first-year writing classes are flagging. The rest of the staff is talking about ways to pique their students' interest (a college-wide reading week, maybe?). Karen and I are wishing ours weren't quite so interested or at least not quite so passionate about voicing their interests. We seem to have a revolt on our hands. The complaints? That our syllabus offers only one perspective; that it is political, that it is leftist, that it is Marxist, that it is not literary enough.

I tell this tale at a dinner party with colleagues who teach biology and political science. Kaye Edwards is amazed that students are so engaged in the course, that they care so intensely about what they are asked to read. Steve Salkever offers me—as possible antidote—Peter Elbow's "The Pedagogy of the Bamboozled":

> There is a crucial contradiction in the role of almost every institutional teacher that prevents our being genuine allies of the student: we are both credit-giver and teacher...few of us, because of our temperaments and because of our institutional setting, are in a position to offer [liberatory pedagogy]...But we can...refrain from bamboozling students. For most of us this would involve making statements such as the following: "This is a course I am giving. I have chosen the materials...decisions about grades and credit are unilaterally mine...We are not studying your lives here...We are not trying to change the world." (88, 93, 94)

This is helpful. I show the essay to my students, remembering their objections to my "double messages": on the one hand, I invite them to speak their own truth, to "voice their voice"; on the other, I manage the discussion and grade the papers according to standards I (and my colleagues) set. I'm going to try to be clearer, more honest, in the future, about which portions of our common work I intend to control.

Otherwise, though, I really don't take Elbow's advice. Instead, I hold extra conferences. I extend class for an hour, to review the history of the course, the complaints about it, and my responses (the "other" perspective is implied; you're certainly not required to accept the one this class explores). And I offer the students some options: remembering that the dissatisfactions of some are the satisfactions of others, trusting the process (even Hegel, whom they loathed, has proved useful to some) and making some changes in the syllabus (cutting down on the overtly political reading, adding some poetry, for instance).

We replace two books with a sequence of love poems (Petrarch, Shakespeare, Rich), and I conduct a discussion about the evolution of a traditional genre. We add Tompkins's and Elbow's essays to the pedagogical material we're reviewing for the last class. I invite additional suggestions for re-working the course next year.

Fall 1992: I put many of them into practice. I include some student papers in the new syllabus. I remove the texts that I didn't enjoy reading or that didn't provoke much reaction from the students and add lots of new ones that expand on the central issues raised by the course: What difference does point of view make? How can we best come to understand those who are different from ourselves? How to distinguish a story from a theory, concrete from abstract? I'm still working very much within the framework Susan Dean established, but now I'm making the course my own. I see it as my version of her vision:

"Points of View/Points of Departure"
Belenky, "Connected Teaching"
Elbow, "The Pedagogy of the Bamboozled"
Coles, "Stories and Theories"
Sacks, "The Man Who Mistook His Wife for a Hat" and
"The World of the Simple"
Bruner, "Two Modes of Thought"
Luria, "Thinking"
Faulkner, "Pantaloon in Black"

Wideman, "Our Time"
Hurston, *Their Eyes Were Watching God*
Percy, "The Loss of the Creature"
Bowles, "A Distant Episode," "Africa Minor,"
"The Time of Friendship," "Allal!"
Geertz, "Thick Description"
Bohannan, "Shakespeare in the Bush"
Carr, "The Historian and His Facts"
Woodham-Smith, *The Reason Why*
Tompkins, "'Indians,' Textualism, Morality and the Problem of History"
Silko, "Language and Literature from a Pueblo Indian Perspective"
Kuhn, *The Structure of Scientific Revolutions*
Fish, "How to Recognize a Poem When You See One"
Whitman, "Song of Myself"
Dickinson, Poems #49, 219, 249, 280, 448, 465, 754, 1129, 1207, 1461, 1651
Scholes, "The Left Hand of Difference"
LeGuin, *The Left Hand of Darkness*
LeGuin, "Is Gender Necessary? Redux"
Blake, *Songs of Innocence and Experience*

Spring 1993: Rather than beginning the semester with colonialist interpretations of *The Tempest,* I ask the class to read the play (with help from successive generations of critics) from Prospero's, then Miranda's, then Caliban's point of view. I'm trying to help the students see that each generation re-reads texts from its own perspective, with an eye to questions that are central to its own time period. I also add more literary texts, and more texts by women; both I and my students like fiction that speaks about our lives:

Dickens, *Great Expectations*
Shakespeare, *The Tempest*
Traversi, "The Tempest"
Fiedler, "The World Without a West"
Kahn, "The Providential Tempest and the Shakespearean Family"
Leininger, "The Miranda Trap"
Orgel, "Prospero's Wife"

Lamming, "The Occasion for Speaking"
Cudjoe, "Jamaica Kincaid and the Modernist Project"
Kincaid, *Annie John*
Rodriguez, *Hunger of Memory*
Cisneros, "From a Writer's Notebook" and *The House on Mango Street*
Gould, selections from *The Mismeasure of Man*
Hegel, "Lordship and Bondage"
Cobb and Sennett, *The Hidden Injuries of Class*
Schneider, "'Our Failures Only Marry'"
Dribben, "Education Was Her Only Escape"
Emerson, "The American Scholar"
Mead, "The Self"
Fuller, "Woman in the Nineteenth Century"
LeGuin, "Bryn Mawr Commencement Address, 1986"
Ruddick, "Maternal Thinking"
Woolf, Chapters 1 and 6, *A Room of One's Own*
Rich, "When We Dead Awaken: Writing as Re-Vision"
Shakespeare, Sonnets 18, 55, 73, 116, 130
Rich, "Twenty-One Love Poems"
Berger, *Ways of Seeing*
DuPlessis, "For the Etruscans," "Sub Rosa," "The Pink Guitar"
Freire, Chapter 2, *Pedagogy of the Oppressed*
Belenky and Elbow again

This year is even harder than the last. Although the students don't complain about the syllabus, they find its insistent focus on issues they face in their own lives difficult to handle; it forces a number of them to ask questions they would rather not examine. It's emotionally draining work for them—and me.

Several students complain that I'm too "rigorous," too "harsh." I find that I need to think more carefully about how I speak to students as vulnerable as these. For those who come from backgrounds of abuse or have had experiences of academic failure, it is very easy to hear my criticism and much harder to hear my praise. The difference in our perceptions is made clear to me in a conference with my strongest student. We are reviewing my comments on her paper: to me, they seem very positive, but she is crying because they seem so critical. When some students ask for models of writing, for examples of "what I want," I photocopy some of the better papers. Other students complain: they feel put down by the comparison.

I stumble across an article by Wendy Luttrell that speaks to their condition. Her research shows that acknowledging and validating some students over others makes the latter feel "unconnected and unknown," "betrayed." Teachers' relationships with their "pets" allow "some students to 'feel special' at the expense of others." It's Luttrell's contention that "what is most memorable about schooling is not what is learned, but how we learn," that "attending to the ethics and politics of relationships is what makes a difference in education" (539–541).

I feel that she's right. I know that she's right. But these relationships can be tricky to negotiate. Some of my students, I think, have come to care too much about my opinion of their work. Because they see that I care very much about them, because they like me so much, they don't want to let me down. They can't write their papers, for fear of disappointing me with work that isn't "good enough."

There are sharp disagreements among the students, too. One woman objects to what seems to her the inauthentic use of academic discourse in the class: "I have heard so much bullshit in this room." Others are angry; they feel that their halting attempts to speak a new and difficult language are being mocked. A student observes that we are learning to work, not just individually as critical thinkers but together, as a group in which we all need to help one another. Freire describes the ideal we're working toward:

> The teacher [and] the students...become jointly responsible for a process in which all grow...The students...are now critical co-investigators in dialogue with the teacher...The pursuit of full humanity...[can be carried out] only in fellowship and solidarity...No one can be authentically human while he prevents others from being so. (*Pedagogy of the Oppressed* 77, 68, 73)

I begin reading more systematically about pedagogy. I come across a definition of "radical teacher," which seems a good description of the kind of classroom experience I am trying to offer, of the kind of teacher l want to be:

> one who respects students...Radical teachers possess the capacity to listen well and the self-control not to always fill silence with the sound of their own voices...Radical teachers are concerned with process as much as product... radical-teaching is holistic; it assumes that minds do not exist separate from bodies and that... thought grows out of lived experience...that people have made different life choices and teach and learn out of a corresponding number of perspectives...Radical teachers demand a lot from their students...Radical teachers do not assume they know it all. (Annas, 340–341)

The hardest part in putting these commitments to work is acknowledging that the students won't always (won't generally) see the world, the texts, the class the way I do. Tompkins's experience, again, is mine: "I'd expected celebration, mutual congratulation, fond reminiscence. What they did was criticize...'There were sixteen rooms in that room'...sixteen different experiences...sixteen different stories going on simultaneously" (*Life* 176, 175). Like Tompkins, I find myself judging my success as a teacher by the evaluation and performance of my students. But they don't always perform as we would wish:

> When I embarked on my experiments in teaching, I thought I was putting the performance mentality behind me by putting students at the center of things. But now I see that the experiment itself became my performance. Only now my success or failure depends on the performance of the students. The ego's need to be reflected *one way or the other* intrudes everywhere. (*Life* 162–163)

I find myself wanting to move beyond that position. Do I care too much about these students? Am I too involved in their lives? But it seems that the only way I can teach now is by entering into relationship with them. (And with their teachers. A perk of working with the non-traditional students has been talking with Susan Dean about our shared syllabus, similar students, similar concerns, similar pedagogy. I've had more conversations in the past three years about what goes on in my classroom than I had in the thirteen years previous. I'm so delighted with our relationship that I suggest to JoEllen Parker, who directs the first-year writing program, that she institutionalize it among other members of the staff. But how? By inviting them to read this journal?)

I'm coming slowly to see that the rubric that best describes what I'm trying to do, the term I like better than either "feminist" or "radical," is that of "Quaker teacher." I've found much support for the kind of work I do in Quaker books and talks: from Parker Palmer, who insists that the essential structure of reality is communal, that "education is a practice of relatedness" (*To Know as We Are Known* 52, 122, 11); from Paul Lacey, who speaks of teachers "guided by the notion that our students are our fellow seekers, companions with a common purpose," and writes of the Quaker perception that there is a teacher in every soul (*Education and the Inward Teacher* 4, 14); and from Mary Rose O'Reilley (a Catholic Quaker), who says that the teacher's primary role is one of focused attention, of being present, of deep, mindful listening. A conference sponsored by Friends' Association for Higher Education confirms these ideas: Sterling Olmstead speaks of our "helping each other into knowing"; at a conference sponsored by Bryn Mawr College's Friends' Association for Higher Education, Carol McCormack describes the "process of developing in the loving company of others."

My evolution as a teacher began by focusing on the careful reading of texts, which I was taught as a grad student in English and still teach to my students under the aegis of the English Department. But I'm arriving now at a recognition that the class itself and the students in it are worthy of the same attentiveness and care. As Tompkins observes,

> all our teaching, what we do in class day after day, is a text—beautiful, strange, many-layered, frightening—woven out of the memory and desire of every person in the room. We never look at this tapestry, almost. It hangs there on our collective mental wall, oscillating gently, sinister, inviting. Its brilliant, darkly textured is world worth the risk of entering, despite the danger. Let's get lost. (*Life* 163)

The adventure of learning to read this text that is the class has been, for me, not one of loss, but of finding—of learning to focus on my students as I once (and still) focus on the texts I bring to them.

Summary comments seem inappropriate for this sequence, which I like to imagine as continually moving. But perhaps a passage from the seventeenth-century Quaker Isaac Penington works well as the last piece I want to paste, just now, in my collage/collegium:

> Our life is love, and peace, and tenderness; and bearing one with another and forgiving one another, and not laying accusations one against another; but praying for one another, and helping one another up with a tender hand. (168)

Fountain. Cloisters. Bryn Mawr College.
Photograph by Carlos Garcia. 2001

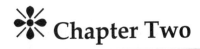 **Chapter Two**

"Outside the Mainstream"/In the "Well of Living Waters": Class as Quaker Meeting for Business

Religious...conceptions of women's liberation...are outside the mainstream of contemporary feminist theorizing. (10)
Alison Jaggers,
Feminist Politics and Human Nature, 1983

There is an aspect of our vocation that is sacred...our work is...to share in the intellectual and spiritual growth of our students...[to] teach in a manner that respects and cares for [their] souls. (13)
bell hooks, *Teaching to Transgress*, 1994

Using these two observations as markers, I'd say that over a ten-year period the language of feminist critics took a "spiritual turn." Kathryn Bond Stockton, who traces this trajectory in some detail in *God Between Their Lips*, explains the current use of spiritual language as a postmodern development, an exploration of a discourse that "exceeds human sign systems" (7–8). Stockton argues, for instance, that the French philosopher Luce Irigaray might powerfully be read "as a feminist theologian of lack" (27). God, in Irigaray's a/theology, designates what we long for, and have not: "'God,' by this logic, *becomes spacing*, 'God' is the gap" (33). Irigaray uses mystical language to evoke the possibility of transcendence, of moving beyond: "a god is necessary: *guaranteeing the infinite*" ("Divine Women" 61).

Stockton's interest is in Irigaray's "spiritualizing" treatment of material bodies. I am using her work here as entry into another line of inquiry altogether, one directed to the gathering of such bodies in the classroom and the possibilities that might open for them if we conceptualize what happens there not merely in spiritual terms but in religious ones—that is, in language most commonly used to describe institutionalized forms of spiritual practice (Stockton xv). I would like to posit the classroom as another long-neglected site of and for religious discourse.

Ten years ago, Janice Raymond identified the "profound religious dimension" of women's studies: "it raises questions of 'ultimate concern,'" has a "unifying function" in women's lives, and offers "transcendent possibilities" of "promise and presence," of "revelatory power" (54–57). Raymond was suggesting then that the work we do in women's studies classes could make the same kinds of promises and have the same kind of effect as work in the religious sphere. I want to suggest now something more than that analogous relationship between religion and feminism. Conceptualizing and articulating in religious terms the work we do in our classrooms may make new contributions to our understanding of what we do as feminist teachers as well as offer us concrete models of how to put into practice feminist ways of knowing and being in the world.

Such work has already been initiated by bell hooks, who uses the words "sacred," "spiritual," and "soul" to describe her classroom presence and practice. hooks draws heavily on the work of the liberatory educator Paulo Freire, whose religious convictions, Ann Berthoff observes, are often neglected by teachers who embrace the political aspects of his pedagogy (237). hooks also writes out of the religious tradition of Buddhism. She frames her book on pedagogy, *Teaching to Transgress*, with a pair of Buddhist practitioners. In her first chapter, hooks describes the "engaged Buddhism" of the Vietnamese monk Thich Nhat Hanh: his "focus on practice in conjunction with contemplation," his emphasis on "a union of mind, body and spirit" (14). hooks ends her book with a passage taken from a journal of Buddhist thought that describes teachers as models who step "outside of the conventional mind" and so prepare their students for "groundlessness" (206–207). In between these descriptions of Buddhist teachers, hooks evokes other, related terms; she counsels professors, for instance "to practice compassion" as they guide students into new paradigms for learning, to recognize and value the presence of each student in the classroom; she describes, as well, the "particular knowledge that comes from suffering" (42, 186, 91).

Like bell hooks, I have come to see that my pedagogical practice is deeply informed by my own religious tradition. In this essay, I want to give testimony, to bear witness to the ways in which my religious practice, that of the Society of Friends, has helped me make sense of and is helping me overcome some of the difficulties I've been led into by the practice of feminist pedagogy, difficulties that center largely on the relations of authority in the classroom.

In part because I have been reluctant to go public with my religious leadings in an academic setting, this process of understanding has been a slow and laborious one. I am offering here a report of my strugglings to put my religious beliefs into practice in the classroom in hope both of re-calling contemporary American feminist theory to one of its neglected roots in Christian theology and of sharing some concrete pedagogical strategies that have grown out of that religious ground. I trace my religious/pedagogical history here in expectation that it may also function as an invitation to feminist teachers, who operate out of other religious traditions and in other pedagogical contexts, to similar reflection.

This chapter has four parts: 1) a description of a central pedagogical issue facing feminist teachers, that of locating and enacting authority in the classroom; 2) an account of the religious authority claimed by early feminists; 3) a review of the Quaker process of group "discernment," of Quaker teaching practices that employ it, and of the dangers and limitations of constructing a community on this model; and finally 4) an offering of a mode of pedagogy drawn from Quaker business practice. In each stage of this account, while working toward the construction of a "feminist

Quaker pedagogy," I acknowledge the difficulties involved in the process. I end, however, by staking a positive claim: that a Quaker notion of religious authority, with its paradoxical links to principles of humility, correctability, communal need, and responsibility, can help us reconceptualize how feminists might teach, and change our practice.

All of the feminist pedagogical theory I've read has been written by teachers, with the usual focus "on the teacher and her methods rather than on students and how they learn" (Dunn 40). In each section of this essay, my words and those of the Quakers and teachers who guide me emerge in response to those of my students, who do a large part of the speaking here, explaining (in letters they've agreed to share) how this process has failed to work, is beginning to work, and still needs working on for them. Their probing, their questioning, their challenging of the project we are undertaking together has brought forth these reflections. I write them in gratitude to, in honor of, and in hopes of responding to the "possibilities"—"that of God"—which each of them represents to me.

"Tearning": Locating Authority in the Classroom

Several years ago, I supervised an independent study of feminist theory and pedagogy by a student, Alisa Conner, who discovered, in the thesaurus,

> that teaching and learning are listed as antonyms of each other…[and] decided to invent a new word that combines them in a way that can express what [we] mean by "feminist pedagogy" in a less jargon-ridden way: "tearning." Said out loud, it sounds like "turning"…and evokes our efforts to turn, shift and change the world. (51)

Although Bryn Mawr College was founded by Quakers, the vision that has guided it for the past hundred years is a rigorously secular one. The mode is hierarchical, with a heavy emphasis on ranking, on bracing academic challenges, on stiff grading standards. Yet because it is a small school with small classes and because I am granted the luxury to structure my own classes as I see fit, I have had the opportunity to experiment here with various forms of feminist liberatory pedagogy. Through a long and circuitous process, I've been trying to position myself and my students in line with Alisa's "tearn," to work together toward a shared understanding, to fulfill the ideal of the teacher who is a joint learner with her students. My early attempts to set up my classrooms as conversations among "equals" led me, however, into belated recognition both of the complex subjectivities my students bring into classes with them and of the insistent dynamics of institutionalized authority that structure our inter-actions with each other.

For some time, I have been beginning each new course by explaining that the knowledge each of us brings to class is incomplete and insufficient, always requiring the balance of the knowledge of others (Luke and Gore 7). I draw in those introductory talks on Frances Maher's definition of feminist methodology as challenging "the validity of any single ...framework," and on her suggestion that we conceptualize knowledge "as a comparison of multiple perspectives" (33–34). I institute a number of rules intended to enable us to put that theory into practice in our discussions: each student must speak in each class to give her own particular "perspective" on the readings, to "balance" what has already been said, but she also must take care not to speak too much, so as to give others equal access to speaking.

Over the years, my students have helped me see the difficulties of enacting such a methodology and such an epistemology in this particular institutional setting, for such practices don't take into adequate account either the competitive and individualistic expectations that they bring to their classes or the institutionalized nature of our respective roles (Weiler 460). One of these students, Jeni A, described in a letter to me her experiences in both male- and female-led classrooms embedded in institutionalized power structures, experiences inflected by her understanding of the ways in which her subjectivity has been constructed. Hers is an account of resistance to my "feminist" pedagogy, grounded in what hooks calls "the passion of remembrance" (90):

I have felt more comfortable with the power dynamic in classes taught by men precisely because they had some sort of power over me...because they tended to teach in a more structured and strict manner. I liked and accepted the hierarchy. Classes taught by women felt more like group therapy sessions where everyone could get their say in, and...relied too heavily on students' personal experience...I had minimal trouble in classes full of women taught by men because I was never shy about expressing myself. (When there were men in the class, however, this changed.)

SO: no holds barred...In our class, when I heard you repeatedly asking me to "hush," make room for others, raise my hand, etc., I felt like the tone was that of an angry mother...A woman was telling me, "Hey, look out for your sisters." That never happened in classes taught by men. I guess I already felt guilty or felt that I monopolized class discussion at times. The comments you made kicked me back twenty years. I heard my mother...calling me down—shaming me, and that made me feel inadequate...I most certainly possess a mean competitive streak, but my feelings of competition that kick in when I'm in front of a class have more to do with wanting attention and approval than anything. (Back to Mom, again.) The primary premise I took from studying religious ritual and identity is that group identification leads to sense of self—and...groups must define themselves over and against another group. Example: I'm a talker against non-talkers in classes. I feel important and strong by defining myself against people who I (and I hate to admit it) see as weaker...The only thing I learned from Foucault is that the power dynamic is constantly in flux—a rather empowering idea, but it means that in every relationship, someone is oppressing or causing fear to someone else...you had power over me, because you were my professor and because I was afraid of you...

I was using my authority, certainly, to force Jeni A into silence, and so to make space for others to speak; I was also trying to use it to get others, as invested in being quiet as she was in talking, to contribute to our discussion. But in explaining to me that she preferred her own speaking to be set off by the silence of her classmates, Jeni A reminded me of her complex notions of self, arrived at in relationship with her mother, myself and other teachers and by measuring her performance against that of her peers. She demonstrated in her letter postmodern conceptions of "identity": "a play of multiple, fractured aspects of the self; it is relational...it is retrospective...[it] is made of successive identifications" (Braidotti 9).

I had hoped to help students like Jeni A learn to speak less as competitive individuals involved in a struggle for power and voice than as members of a community seeking understanding together. In doing so, I was refusing the counsel of a number of postmodern feminist philosophers. Mimi Orner, for instance, dispenses altogether with such a project. Arguing that our "attempt to empower students to find and articulate their voices" is "a controlling process," Orner dismisses "genuine sharing of voice in the classroom" as "impossibly naïve" (87, 81). Insisting similarly that feminist teachers "leave intact the institutionalized power imbalances between themselves and their students, the essentially paternalistic project of education itself, and the authoritarian nature of the teacher/student relationship," Elizabeth Ellsworth likewise concludes that our classes can only begin to work together through a mutual concession that all our knowings are and always will be not just "partial, interested" but "potentially oppressive to others" (98, 115).

The work of Orner and Ellsworth has been helpful to me in making sense of what they call the "oppressive moments" in teaching practice. But the methods I'm evolving for dealing with such moments, my attempts at restructuring my classroom so that they can at least be made useful, differ from those they describe. I think that it is possible to use our "partial" knowledges to construct a shared understanding that can be transformative. I try to do so by drawing on an alternative theory that calls attention not to the teacher's institutional authority, which is the locus of Orner and Ellsworth's attention, but rather to an authority that can be constructed by the group that gathers in the classroom. That theory taps sources that neither Orner nor Ellsworth considers: religious ways of knowing.

Joan Scott describes experience as a "linguistic event" that "doesn't happen outside established meanings" (34); Judith Butler argues similarly that identity is not "a simple injunction to become who or what I already am," but rather "a production...usually in response to a request" (*Inside/Out* 13). In line with such thinking, I have been moved to extend to Jeni A and her fellow students a new "identity category," one drawn from the "regulatory regime" we call religion (*Inside/Out* 13). I now offer my students the language of religion to describe the experience of what happens in our classes, in hopes that it might open us to new possibilities. If we are willing to experiment with "the categories" in which we identify ourselves, we may be able to change "with them possibilities for thinking the self" (Joan Scott 35).

Risk: Seeking Religious Authority

> if anything divine is still to come our way it will be won by abandoning all control...it is through risk, only risk, leading no one knows where...No project here. (53)
>   Irigaray, "Belief Itself" (1980)

I have come to articulate my feminist pedagogy in specifically religious terms: I try to ground my feminist classrooms in religious principles, conceptualizing my students as companions on a path that has spiritual as well as intellectual dimensions, with all of us moving toward growth and development. I choose to teach texts that reinforce such a conception. In my course on the intellectual history of feminism, students are intrigued to hear the religious authority claimed by early feminists: Anne Hutchinson, Sor Juana Inez de la Cruz, Mary Wollstonecraft, Margaret Fuller, Sojourner Truth (for starters) called on God as their first witness, using the concept of spiritual equality as foundational to their pleas for educational, economic, and political reform.

In tracing the concept of spiritual equality in these early calls for women's rights, I suggest that Quakers—William Penn, Margaret Fox, Sarah Grimke, Lucretia Mott, Susan B. Anthony—are of particular note. The Quaker historian Margaret Bacon observes that "many Quaker values became embedded" in the ideology and practice of the American women's movement in the nineteenth century and calls for the reintroduction of such values "by spiritually-minded women" in the twentieth century: "Feminism, properly understood, is a call for authentic spiritual development, based on the authority of one's own experience of the Light" (2, 229).

But how does such a call play out when the venue is a gender studies classroom at the turn of the twenty-first century, one that both interrogates and acknowledges the notion of the "authority of experience"? Diana Fuss poses the question this way: "How are we to negotiate the gap between the conservative fiction of experience as the ground of all truth-knowledge and the immense power of this fiction to enable and encourage student participation?" (hooks 87)

I begin "negotiating that gap" by first insisting that I and the students each come to class equally able to speak out of our own passionate memories of living and reading, as Jeni A did in her letter. To promote such speaking in the classroom, I ask several students to initiate each session: they meet ahead of time and prepare an agenda, a series of questions for us to consider as a group. In the course of the semester, each of the students writes several analytic papers, which I grade in the conventional ways, but they also consult with me in evaluating other aspects of their course work, both their journals (more recently, recorded in electronic newsgroups) and their contributions to class discussion. At the end of the semester, I invite each student to write an autobiography or the biography of another woman she knows, or to express her understanding of feminism in another form—to make it visible, for instance, in dance, sculpture, painting, quilting—and to grade that final project in accord with standards she sets herself.

Students are always receptive to and grateful for this approach, which attempts to balance conventional academic modes of analysis with what seem to them more "experiential" forms of knowing. But several years ago, when a student I'll call Liz charged me with "betrayal" and refused to take an exam in a course on American writers called "Womanspirit Rising," I asked myself if the invitation I had extended to rely on "the authority of her own experience of the Light" was compatible with my increasing awareness of the social construction of the self, and/or with my—and her—institutional obligations. This was Liz's response to my exam:

THINGS ARE NOT WHAT THEY SEEM.
today i took a walk in the rain and a fire hydrant looked like a small child.

self-development comes only through self-sacrifice. you must give up your life to find it.

a caterpillar is a butterfly hiding.

This College does not exist. It's a construct that people have an agreement on. We will live in these buildings and i will teach you and you will learn from me or pretend to and i will give you a piece of paper that says you were here. it may be a reality in people's lives, but it doesn't exist the way a tree does. that tree is there whether or not we agree that it is. take the agreement away from the college and you have buildings + people milling around.

"Womanspirit Rising" does not exist. it also is a construct because it depends on such constructs as grades, authority, + the college.

WELL, what if i choose not to believe in the construct we call "Womanspirit Rising"? this exam becomes a choice, not an obligation. this exam becomes a spiritual experience. i'm choosing to take it my way

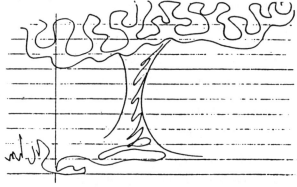

the first day of class you gave us a "koosh" ball to help us learn how to discuss among ourselves. you didn't want us to channel everything back through you. You said you were a fellow-seeker, someone who is looking to learn from the class like we were. you let us present the topics for discussion instead of opening every discussion yourself. you didn't sit at the head of the table. you spoke with us frankly + openly. you had us for dinner at your house. we were really people with each other. you were the most radicalteacher i've ever had. you worked to make the classroom student-based + oriented. you worked for nonauthoritarianism. you showed interest in the process of my spiritual discoveries in my papers. the fact that i didn't come up with an Answer, a Product, didn't concern you. i felt our class had the potential to move towards reality, to *really* exist as people talking + searching together. oh yeah—you let us choose our own grades for our final projects— another step towards NO CONSTRUCTS, LET'S BE REAL.

BUT

you assigned this exam. it seems like a betrayal. a last-minute back-slide into the typical college system. the reason you gave for this exam was that you didn't want your class *SQUEEZED* out. you said in past years the readings never got done, or only half-done because other classes got priority. you didn't want that, so you assigned this exam. and

BOOM

you got yourself a

teacher

_____

student

hierarchy. you asked something of us that you were afraid we wouldn't give + you used your power over our GRADE as a kind of threat. keep us in line. remind us of our position. same thing happened when you said you would take our class participation into consideration when averaging our final grade.

uh oh. ok then i'd better talk. bullshit. suddenly all the dynamics you wanted, of equality + fellow-seekers + such were thrown off. we did really well for a college class, but not good enough for the standards you set. and the standards I wanted.

INTERMISSION

well ladies + gents, have yourself a good stretch, use the bathroom, blah blah blah. i'd like to take this opportunity to make a small disclaimer: you did a good job. like I said, you are the most radical teacher i've ever had. overall, you are to be commended for your thoughtfulness + hard work. i'm just trying to show why i won't take this exam the way you asked me to. and blah blah blah you may take your seats now. one year ago i stood up in front of my high school + families + friends + i gave a valedictory speech + read poetry. i got money + awards for having worked my butt off. i looked out at all the people who were looking at me + i looked at my parents who were proud of me + i looked at the palms of my hands + i regretted the way i'd spent my four years in high school. standing up there, i know i should have asked the hard questions i really wanted to ask, the ones that might not have had answers. i should have taken risks. but i got good grades + i got it done + i got money for it. it stood up there + vowed to myself that i wouldn't do anything for a grade again; that i would live + learn from the inside out; that i would ask the real questions + tell it how it is + not pretend + and not bullshit + take *risks.* i'm taking a risk right now. it's a little scary. it feels good.

the grades you give + this exam i'm taking are betrayals of the standards you set. where's that class on *Moby Dick + Beloved*? i want to take it. it sounds real. why don't you try something like that next year? it is a risk. once the grades + exam are gone, there's nothing you can hold over the students' heads. they will have to drive themselves to learn + grow. you will be, in every sense, a resource, a guide, + fellow-seeker. it could fall through. maybe nobody will come, readings won't get done, + nobody will learn anything. or *maybe,* with nothing to lose, the students will

D

   I

      V

        E

into the material with total abandon + come up SWIMMING in new exciting questions + possible answers. it's worth a try!

my role in this construct is still what's at hand. yes, i could choose to write about what makes a spiritual experience, in my life + based on the women we've read, or the nature of GOD, or pride + humility. i know i have read enough + could write well on any of the topics. which is why i won't do this exam. i don't have to prove anything to myself. i learned a lot process-wise. i don't want to crank out a product so that i can prove to you what should be a given: that i'm a responsible, caring, hardworking student who will learn because she wants to. if this school truly operated on the premise that students are to be trusted and respected, there would be no exam. there would be no need.

I KNOW WHAT I KNOW

My initial reaction to this non-exam exam was one of pleasure, for Liz was here affirming a fundamental premise of Quakerism, the validity of what each of us knows experientially. And yet her going for the prophetic "high ground" also provoked and prodded me to think further about her insistence that she was accountable only to a rarified notion of radical independent selfhood. She did not see herself as accountable to me, who was grading her; to the institution which, eventually, would be giving her a diploma; nor to the larger social constraints in which, and by which, her selfhood had been contructed.

Learning more about the history of Quakerism, about its evolution from the concept of "individual revelation" into an organized religion, and about its current practice as mediated by teachers who understand the academic and religious life as congruent, I began to try out additional ways of structuring my classes to meet both individual and institutional, spiritual and secular demands. I began to find some answers to the questions Liz posed, as I myself came into a more postmodern understanding both of the "self" and of my own religious tradition.

Attention: The Process of Group Discernment

> Prayer consists of attention...the development of the
> faculty of attention [also] forms the real object and almost
> the sole interest of studies. Every school exercise is like a
> sacrament. (105, 112)
>
> > Simone Weil, *Waiting for God* (1964)

Quakerism began in mid-seventeenth-century England with
the "openings," or intuitive perceptions, of George Fox, who was
convinced that the love and power of the divine spirit was present
within every person (Hubbard 15–24). But the early Quakers
distinguished themselves from the other Anabaptist groups, as
Margaret Bacon explains, by meeting regularly, "so that they
might check...to see if one person's sense of a holy leading met a
corresponding answer in the souls of his or her peers," a process
of verification which she calls the "birth of that delicate balance
between individual freedom and group authority...at the heart of
Quakerism" (20). The Quaker educator Paul Lacey describes this
history and its consequences for Quaker practice today:

> Minding and answering are reciprocal, dialogic actions...one way of
> distinguishing the Quaker from the Ranter. The Ranters seized onto the
> absolute freedom of the gospel and insisted that all things were
> permitted to whoever followed...divine inspiration. For them there
> could be no authority outside of the individual's own conviction and
> neither the need nor the means to test the rightness of the individual's
> understanding or motive...but...Friends learned [that]...the commun-
> ity...must practice discernment to test when an individual...was rightly
> led. (*Education and the Inward Teacher* 9)

Richard Bauman draws on the work of Max Weber on the
"routinization of charisma" to trace the process of consolidation
that took place in Quakerism. As the original "ideal of unfettered
prophetic ministry accountable only to direct divine guidance"
was "brought under corporate control," Bauman explains,
Quakerism made a transition to a gathered, disciplined fellowship
(147).

I try now to institute such a fellowship in my classes: more than a call for authentic individual development, which Liz responded to so strongly and so positively, I conceptualize these classes as testings of what seem to be individual "leadings" against both the texts and the leadings of others. Such a pedagogy is in accord with current thinking on the role that "social constraint" plays in the "processes of identity production," which insists that it is not "individuals who have experience, but subjects who are constituted" through it (Joan Scott 25–26).

The Quaker educator Parker Palmer uses the Quaker practice of worship as a model for the work that I try to encourage in my classroom. In his pamphlet "Meeting for Learning," Palmer describes a religious version of the social construction of meaning, in which our partial understandings serve as the ground of our need for and usefulness to one another:

> The teacher [like] a thoughtful host establishes an atmosphere...to nurture and encourage the expertise of others in a meeting for learning [the individual is always in relationship,] and knowledge emerges in dialogue...learning happens between persons. (2–4)

I have a number of different ways of encouraging this kind of conversation. For instance, when a student finishes speaking, she is asked to call on another student rather than expect me either to comment or to referee the observations that follow hers. Each student is asked to try to respond, not only to the text but also to the student whose speaking has preceded her own. So—although I ask leading questions in order to nudge the conversation forward or for purposes of clarification—it becomes the obligation of each student to make what she says useful to the group.

Palmer dubs this process a "meeting for learning." Another Quaker teacher, Mary Rose O'Reilley, describes it as a "peaceable classroom," for it teaches

> students to respect each other...to attend to that of wisdom in each contribution. To listen thus attentively, to question thus seriously, is not to undermine authority but to increase sensitivity to its authentic voice...I have come to distrust any pedagogy that does not conclude in the communal: subject to the checks and balances of the others, the teacher, the tradition, and the texts. (*The Peaceable Classroom* 23, 60–61)

The work of these Quaker educators focuses less on the "democratic" nature of the classroom than on the need for each class member to practice "attentiveness," first to the texts, to evidence that will support her claims, but also to what her classmates have to say and to how her contribution fits in with the larger conversation. I try to model such attentiveness for the group by listening carefully to each comment each student makes, not turning from a labored or halting articulation, for instance, to check the text or the time or my own agenda for what we need to be covering during the hour. I try to direct the attention of my students similarly when it seems to wander.

I see myself now as a guide who helps to structure a conversation, to make its pattern explicit, but not to direct it; lately, I've given over the structuring as well. In a course I taught a few years ago, the group of twenty-five was too large for a conversation in which all could participate. I asked small groups of students both to prepare initial questions and to decide on the format in which they would be discussed: Did they want to break up into small groups, stage a debate, have us move around the room to "mark" our changing responses to a given issue, even hand out lollipops or fruit as incentives to participation? They tried such tactics—and others that never would have occurred to me. But the format was always in accord with the Quaker practice of public testing:

> Whatever insight one thinks one has…must be put forward publicly and tested against the knowledge of the group. And the individual must feel the weight of the group's response to what he or she has offered…It is part of the genius of Quakerism, I think, that the movement of the spirit [and of the intellect] is not enclosed as a private matter, but is made manifest in public ways and put to public test. (Palmer, "Meeting" 4, 6)

The director of our First-Year Writing program and the Bryn Mawr College Appointments Committee have suggested that there are important differences between the act of becoming a member of a Quaker meeting and that of enrolling in one of my feminist classrooms. I would like to answer that both "memberships" involve an "acceptance of responsibility and sense of commitment" to a shared process (Hubbard 214). But many students come to college because it is socially accepted and because they are expected to do so. When they enroll in my courses, not in search of self-fulfillment, as Liz did, but to fulfill graduation requirements, I can hardly assume that they will be committed to the discipline of group discernment.

There are many other reasons why students might not be able to participate fully in one of my classes. Not only those who take issue with my philosophical or pedagogical principles, but those who have, for example, experienced a death in the family, are suffering from depression or are just having a hard time of it, find it difficult to be present when we are insistently making sure, each Tuesday and Thursday afternoon, that we are "all there," all actively participating in a common learning project. My Quaker feminist pedagogy does enforce a certain "presence" and with it perhaps a certain sameness in attitude: in engagement, in energy, in willingness to have one's insights be tested always against those of the group.

I may be asking for a commitment that some of my students are not able to make, and assuming a shared sense of values which I cannot reasonably assume. Such an assumption was certainly not fulfilled in a course I taught several years ago called "New Patterns in Feminist Spirituality." I brought to the class all I knew at the time about feminist and critical pedagogies; I struggled with new texts along with the students, trying to be open to a variety of perspectives, a variety of experiences, a variety of readings. The course was, generally, a successful one, but it did not work well for two roommates, quiet students who took their Christian faith very seriously, who found the whole notion of testing multiple readings and multiple "truths" against one another threatening and disruptive.

When I tried to give space to religious understanding in the classroom, one of those religious student lost her balance. Was that because I encouraged "religious talk" only in the context of multiplicities of truth, of social constructions of meaning, in ways that seemed threatening to a young Christian? When I attempted to make what was central to this student's life, her sense of Spirit, central to the classroom, she described herself as being on a different "wavelength" from me, as feeling "boxed in" by my teaching methods. It seemed to her that I had constructed a "game" she didn't know how—and *didn't want to learn* how—to "play," a game whose "rules" appeared to her nonsensical.

My approach may not be helpful—may actually do harm—to students whose educational expectations, religious beliefs or cultural practices are different from my own. A more various population than the one I teach might test even more fully the limits of my methods. In some Native American cultures, for instance, eye contact is seen as rude and public speaking as inappropriate. It would certainly be a violation of such customs to enforce, in my classrooms, a religious practice that requires everyone to speak.

My colleague Chris Castiglia has suggested to me that my process "works" (in so far as it works!) only because the members of my classes have been pre-selected to conform. The homogenizing context of my classroom is made possible, he says, by an admissions office that weeds out those who are dramatically uncomfortable with their subject positions as well as those who challenged pedagogical authority too stringently in the past. By the time they get to me, students are usually fairly articulate in speaking and in writing, and—more importantly for the purposes of this argument—insistently well socialized into acceptable practices for classroom discussion.

By requiring that everyone speak and by insisting that they speak with a consciousness of how their observations work with those of the group as a whole, I may be encouraging students, as they have been encouraged by teachers in the past, to say only what they think the rest of the group will find acceptable and so enforcing a certain conformity. Hilda Kauffman, who was enrolled in a first-year composition and literature course I offered for returning students, explained how the limits of acceptable speech get enforced by the way students have learned to construct themselves as a group. Hilda's paper, written in response to a class discussion of *Jane Eyre,* is entitled

"What is in the Attic of this Classroom?"

...In spite of the "problem-posing" method of teaching, which ideally allows great latitude and "assists us in giving birth to our own ideas" (Belenky et al. 217), we as a group are basically conservative...because this is the way that groups function in order to be stable. And we are also conservative because we are tentative.

Despite the "midwife" teaching climate that Anne has created, we invest her with authority and our perception determines our behavior. We seek to please the teacher...There is no stated way of seeing that she has promoted, but when we talk to each other about the class we try to uncover "what she wants." And we also seek to please the other group members so that they'll accept us and be full-fledged members of the community. As Jane Eyre tells Helen Burns, "I know I should think well of myself; but that is not enough; if others don't love me, I would rather die than live—I cannot bear to be solitary and hated." Jane has a "great delight in pleasing my teachers, especially such as I loved." As new students who have come to this college by circuitous routes, some of us need to prove that we belong here and so feel compelled to sound "smart," which may get in the way of not knowing, of asking provocative or "stupid" questions...When an authority is invested with a great deal of power, questions are carefully, judiciously framed...

In our non-hierarchical classroom, we have no overt limits on the unusualness of our ideas...But we do have limits. The interpretive community constructs a group identity. Who are we then? In this classroom we begin to interpret our individual lives through the norms of the group...We say [that *Jane Eyre* is a great novel] because within its story we can interpret ourselves, find ourselves through the text: nuances of our feelings, identification of our passion, our rage, our sexuality and our oppression...

But Jane is not the only character with whom we might identify. Bertha Rochester's tortured existence leads me to the question: who is the Mad Woman in our classroom, or perhaps, more interestingly, where is the attic that contains our outrageous, provocative thoughts? Charlotte Bronte (and you could say the interpretive community) won't let the Mad Woman speak, won't give her a voice because she's too alarming, too disturbing. (When she spoke in her youth in the West Indies, she screamed profanities.) The underlying danger in any community is that if you go beyond the limits, you will wind up in the attic. Sensing this danger I keep my most peculiar thoughts on the margins...

Perhaps if the group accepts your individuality, your stretching of the boundaries, you too become a privileged knower. If, though, you go too far, cross some fine check-point in the agreed-upon landscape, if your iconoclasm is too extreme, you cross an irrevocable line...The Mad Woman reigns over the attic, the room where the class stockpiles its creativity and risky ideas, its dangerous identities, a forbidden place of laughter and screaming.

Both Chris and Hilda describe my classroom, which I try to construct as a shared struggle toward understanding, as a performance of *the same*, with the apparent "diffusing" of authority among class members as the surest sign of authority's institutionalized—and internalized—operation. The concerns they raise have also been expressed by postmodern feminist philosophers. Mimi Orner, for instance, points to "the hidden curriculum of the 'talking circle'—the long cherished form of the democratic classroom...[as] an expression of disciplinary power—the regulation of the self through the internalization of the regulation by others" (83). Iris Marion Young claims, more generally, that the loss of extremes Hilda describes is the price we pay for community; she argues that we need, instead, "to attend to the irreducibility of difference" (305). I move in another direction, toward the alternative that I see offered by Quaker process: the irreducibility of our need for and responsibility to one another, in the shared construction and, yes, institutionalization of an authority that can be understood and expressed in religious terms.

The "Well of Living Waters": Quaker Business Practice
we...were in some degree baptized into a feeling sense of the
conditions of the people...the well of living waters was at
times opened, to our encouragement and...refreshment. (37)
The Journal of John Woolman (1743–1748)

Some years ago, I took a month-long course at my
meetinghouse on the topic of eldering, in which the instructor,
Kenneth Sutton, tried to update for us an old Quaker notion. The
idea he developed for us was two-fold: that each of us has the
responsibility and the authority to speak up when something in
Meeting disturbs us, that we should not wait for a "weighty
Friend" to do the speaking for us. But—and this is the flip side of
the same coin—each of us needs to cultivate a sense of humility,
knowing that we can also be corrected by others. I understand
now that the two ideas depend absolutely on one another: we can
express with authority the "truth" as we see it in a given moment,
knowing that our speaking will provoke others with different
viewpoints to correct us. We can feel free to speak, because we
know that we will be corrected, that revision is always possible,
indeed always necessary. Correcting people is okay, can even be a
calling if rightly fulfilled, as long as we hold ourselves open to
correction as well. Susan Bordo explains the process in
postmodern secular and political terms: "It is impossible to be
'politically correct'... all ideas...are condemned to be haunted by a
voice from the margins...awakening us to what has been
excluded, effaced, damaged...this is, of course, the way we learn"
(138, 154).

All of the students who speak in this essay raise questions
about the relationships of authority played out in my classrooms.
Jeni A fretted about my authority to enforce her silence, Liz about
my refusal to grant her the authority to decide for herself what she
needed to know. Hilda described the similar authority of the class
to censor itself, to place limits on what is said in the group. I am
trying to answer such queries now with a theory of authority that
is religious in nature, trying to re-configure my classrooms by
drawing, not just generally on Quaker theology, which suggests

that we "walk mindfully over the earth, answering that of God in everyone" (Fox 93), but specifically on Quaker business practice.

Helen Hole explains the traditional position on governance. If "in each person, there is some element of the Divine, and therefore some potential for access to the Truth," authority will not be entrusted to any single individual. In Meeting for Business, rather, agreement grows "out of the pooling and sharing" of those involved; the aim is "to discover the Truth, which will satisfy everyone." Quakers believe that such satisfaction is possible, for our "deepest self is one which touches that of others; we belong to the one vine...of which we are all branches" (97–99).

In the "corporate search for Truth" that is Quaker business practice, all members "must accept a kind of vulnerability." They must be willing both to verbalize what they care about and "try to be open to another's point of view, endeavor to understand it, and even think themselves into it" (Hole 99, 102). In *Beyond Majority Rule*, Thomas Brown argues that all participants must be willing to make a spoken contribution: it is of great importance that Friends who feel they cannot speak, "who are diffident about the significance of their share in the Meeting be encouraged to say what they can." James Walker observes that "quiet ones" must accept some blame for decisions made without their imput and that "more vocal Friends" need "temper their remarks in order to encourage reluctant speakers." Howard Brinton encourages all Friends "to express their opinions humbly and tentatively in the realization that no one person sees the "whole Truth and that the whole meeting can see more of Truth than can any part of it" (Sheeran 55–56).

Much of the language of the early Quakers speaks of "keeping low." *The Journal of George Fox* instructs, "All Friends be low, and keep in the life of God to keep you low" (86). His Epistles counsel likewise: "sink down in that which is pure" (10: 129). Such language makes contemporaries (including contemporary Quakers!) uncomfortable. But when Sterling Olmstead suggested recently to a group of Friends' educators that "keeping low" might be a way of directing our attention to our common source, our common root, I began to see that the term "lowness" implies interconnectedness and sympathy. John Woolman, for instance, gives testimony that, as he "was preserved in the ministry to keep low with the Truth, the same Truth in their hearts answered it," that he "often saw the necessity of keeping down to that root from whence our concern proceeded" (63, 96).

Michael Sheeran finds such humility the most striking quality of the Quaker business method: the "tentativeness" of individual speakers, the "artless willingness to face the weaknesses in one's position," the "atmosphere of respectful openness to one another." The atmosphere necessary for this process to work emphasizes "a sense of the partiality of one's own insights, and a dependence on searching together with the group for better conclusions than anyone alone could have attained." The clerk of business meeting needs to exercise thoughtful speaking, attentive listening, and the gift of discernment: "the ability to 'read' the group," to report unity when—and if—it is reached (56, 59, 61, 101).

I am trying now explicitly to institutionalize this religious conception of authority in my classes, by modeling them on the practice of Quaker Meeting for Business. I position myself as clerk, as "reader" of the discussions I direct. Every student in each of my classes, like everyone in business meeting, has an obligation not only to speak but to speak in a certain way—tentatively, and with an awareness of what might be useful for us all. Reflecting on the use of personal experience in the gender studies classroom, Alisa Conner (the first student to speak in this essay) distinguished between inappropriate and uncomfortable "confession" and empowering and publically useful "testimony":

> The language of personal experience turns into "confession" when it becomes self-protective, when it shuts people off from really examining themselves and their discourses…"testimony," in contrast, is "toward something," meaningful to other people as well as to the testified. (29)

Our judgment of what counts as "testimony" is constant, ongoing, evolving, adjustable. It always means careful readings of the texts with attention both to nuances of argument and our vested interests in them; often it means reflecting on classroom dynamics; sometimes it means stories of the choices our mothers have made in their lives or hopes we have for our own.

The obligation to speak—and this is key—is particularly weighty if a student finds herself in disagreement with the general tenor or focus of the conversation. By insisting that students take the responsibility for fulfilling that obligation, I am trying to counter the homogenizing tendency of secular community-building with what seems to me a more religious and more open sense of our common need for understanding, an understanding that will be incomplete unless each of our perspectives, the "access to truth" that each of us represents, is included.

Many quiet students have told me they are grateful that I insist on their speaking: it's a welcome relief, they say, to know that they *must* speak, that I respect them enough to assure them the time and space they need to do so. To speak, they come to acknowledge, is to make themselves vulnerable to critique, but it is also to aid our group work towards comprehension; to refuse to speak is to deny both themselves and others the possibility of being educated.

In establishing the classroom as a site for this particular religious practice, which locates authority in the assumption that, by working together, we can come into a more adequate understanding than each of us could achieve alone, I am continually reminding my students of their obligation to listen carefully to the testimonies of others. Another of my returning students, Lynn Litterine, described her understanding of how this process took place in a course called "Major Texts of the Feminist Tradition":

> What if feminism means listening to the other woman's voice when she talks, instead of our own voice jumping ahead of her with impatience, or with fear, or with prejudice, or with boredom...? What if feminism means a determination to understand women when they speak? Or in their silence?...it would be a listening, a careful listening...but it would be specifically feminist because it would be listening with an awareness of all the barriers to women being really heard, an awareness of all my own handicaps to hearing...when it comes to women, the whole damn world is hearing impaired...I call my plan "Feminism As Hearing Aid."

I'm going to miss this class, because it's a safe place to get to know the other women in the room. Here I can practice listening to another person reveal and explain her thoughts. I can slow down the anxious din in my mind and look and listen...my love and connection were clarified and exercised and I now listen to other women within that strong framework.

I'd like [my graduation] to be Q&A...

Listening one another into speech, testifying in ways that help others hear themselves in the story—or hear their exclusion and so feel called to testify in turn—the touchstone of such teaching is a process of communal "tearning" that involves the principle of correctability, an authority grounded in humility, and an awareness of our shared need for and usefulness to one another. Paulo Freire, who first invited both bell hooks and me into a practice of liberatory pedagogy, reflected more recently on the importance of such a process in academic life. Acknowledging a "scarcity of humbleness" in academia, our "fear of others' intelligence," Freire insisted that tolerance, "giving the testimony of respect to the ways of others," is indispensable to the task of education (The Catholic University). Luce Irigaray, whose interest lies less in the classroom than in the written uses of language, describes a similar interchange, and names it love. She calls it "a style of loving relationships" ("The Three Genders" 177), which plays with the "forever unstable modulation of truth":

The cries...about the "death of God" are a summons for the divine to return as festival, grace, love, thought...the annunciation of another parousia of the divine. Which involves the remolding of...discourse. ("Love of the Other" 14)

Pembroke Dining Room. Bryn Mawr College.
Courtesy of Bryn Mawr College Library.

❋ Chapter Three

"Shuddering Without End":
Class as Dinner Party

Abby Reed, speaking at semester's end
    At our dinner party some heap food on their plates
    and I watch them
    as they cut in line
    finish dessert
    exclaim how delicious everything was
    and lie back, complacently nourished
    and talk of sisterhood and care,
    vaguely conscious that there are many of us
    furiously hungry in the corner.
    It is on the backs of the silent that the few are brought to
    voice.

I wish to talk about silence in our feminist classroom, using the metaphor of the dinner party. I was thinking of several dinner parties when I began this project. One of these was Judy Chicago's collaborative art installation *The Dinner Party*, a massive triangular table with thirty-nine place settings for thirty-nine women, thirty-nine feminist heroes. Another was the dinner party we're attending tonight to mark the end of our gender studies seminar. And yet another was the metaphoric table Anne told me that she used to think about the classroom.

    Anne related an anecdote about one of her students who quit in frustration over the political correctness of her classroom conversations. Anne said that she was "trying to build a table large and steady enough for everyone to sit around, and was devastated that someone had chosen not to stay at the table." Before Anne told me that story, however, I had already begun thinking of our class time as a dinner party, in which some decline their invitation; some wish they had never accepted; some hate the food; some love the food; some love the hostesses; some can't stand the hostesses; some guests are well fed and happily dominate discussion, performing for the other guests; and some sit, hungrily, angrily in the corner, wondering why they've suddenly lost their appetite along with their ability to speak.

I'm in that last group of students, although I haven't lost my appetite—actually, I'm ravenous. I read for class because the texts were, for the most part, genuinely interesting to me; I engaged them and thought about them. But I would enter the classroom and, within the first twenty minutes, would usually be twisting uncomfortably in my seat, every muscle tense, watching the clock and sighing, sometimes more loudly than I realized, waiting for the hour and half to end. I felt deeply angry with many of my classmates, who theorized about an ethic of care yet were perfectly comfortable to speak first and often and long again and again. It is my opinion that we were not attentive to the silent in our classroom, that the loud voices of a few trampled on those of the silent.

I was extremely frustrated with the discussions in our classroom, and Anne kept encouraging me to speak more in class; "feminist pedagogues want to *empower* students to find and articulate their silenced and/or delegitimated voices" (Orner 83). But I never did, never felt able to answer the questions posed or productively intervene once discussion had begun. Throughout this process, I never doubted my intelligence or my ability to engage these texts. But I did wonder where my voice had gone and why certain women in our class felt able to speak almost all the time. I began to notice that there were other class members who never spoke either, that I literally had no idea what their voices sounded like, their intonation and pitch and what in the world they might be thinking. I began to notice their different resistances, and I know that there were other resistances I did not notice.

I noticed the students who came to class after our opening moment of silence, the students who wouldn't come to class when we were doing movement exercises, the students who would just miss a lot of classes (perhaps with a pattern?), the students whose crossed arms and sullen expressions could be read many ways but who would never verbally articulate their fierce anger in the classroom.

Why did some women feel so comfortable dominating class discussion, and why was that permitted? In a discussion outside of class, one of our classmates said to me, "I don't mean to silence you, but" and continued to speak for several more minutes. I was astonished. "I don't mean to silence you but" seemed to be exactly what was happening in our classroom even while we claimed an "ethic of care." In the feminist classroom, I have been taught that women's voices are valuable, yet we did not value every individual voice in the classroom.

Judy Chicago's *The Dinner Party* and our class similarly attempt to bring the voiceless, the unheard, to voice. Each of the thirty-nine place settings "commemorates a goddess, historic personage, or important woman" (Chicago 3). These women heroes should be as familiar "to us" as male heroes, according to Chicago, and they should be equally commemorated. She claims that the female heroes seated at the table and those whose names are inscribed on the *Heritage Floor* are equally worthy of commemoration as well, yet she writes that "the lustred porcelain surface" of the *Heritage Floor* "serves as the foundation for *The Dinner Party* table and the many important human accomplishments it symbolizes" (Chicago 3). These women on the *Heritage Floor* are not the canonized feminist heroes who get to attend the "dinner party"; instead, they are credited for enabling the women at the dinner party to get their invitations. Those at the dinner party benefited from the status of those on the floor, from thoughts and accomplishments that were not deemed worthy of status at the party. They are the foundation, inscribed on the floor, hungry and walked upon.

In a similar manner, the silent, voiceless majority in our class acts as the audience for those few who speak in class, those who own the class, to whom the class really belongs. The silent are present in the classroom; they turn in papers and (sometimes obligatorily) meet with Anne and her co-teacher Kaye and (sometimes reluctantly) turn in their e-mail reports, so in this way their voices inevitably weave their way into discussion. Yet their voices are co-opted when they are forced into discussion by a professor. I would tell them of my conversations with my friends, our almost daily angry, hilarious, furious conversations about the class, but I was still unable to speak in class. Once I spoke angrily in class, once on the newsgroup; a few times I was called on, and once or twice I spoke on my own. As Ira Shor observes, students "talk a lot among themselves, but grow quiet in the presence of authorities. To talk a lot in an institution, at work, at school or in front of superiors...is to be guilty of collaborating with the enemy" (qted. in Orner 88).

I am not positing Anne and Kaye as the enemy. Different from Shor's formulation, I grew silent in the authority of our "talking circle" rather than in the presence of our professors. Orner writes that the talking "circle," the "long-cherished form of the democratic classroom" is an expression of disciplinary power, in which subjects "internalize systems of surveillance to the point that we become our own overseer." The fear and knowledge of constant surveillance calls for "the regulation of the self through the internalization of the regulation by others." Orner writes that the calls for student voice in the talking circle and the calls for testimony encourage confession "in the presence of authority figures such as teachers" (83).

But who was the authority in the classroom? A few students dominated discussion and silenced their peers. Anne and Kaye allowed them to dominate and then co-opted the voices of the silent in an acknowledgment and acceptance of their domination. It is on the backs of the silent that these few are brought to voice. In the attempt to bring the members of our class to voice, a demand for student voice—as Gayatri Spivak wrote in "Can the Subaltern Speak?"—welcomed "selective inhabitants of the margin in order to better exclude the margin."

Voice is not static; it is socially determined. I will not "get my voice back" by doing this project. But as Margo Culley, feminist pedagogy theorist, wrote, "Anger is a challenging and necessary part of life in the feminist classroom" (216), and this anger should be "felt and acknowledged, not denied." Here I am, angry. As Culley quotes the narrator of Toni Morrison's *The Bluest Eye,* "Anger is better. There's a sense of being in anger, an awareness of worth. It is a lovely surging" (Culley 216).

—Abby Reed, May 4, 1998

Anne, describing the preparations for the party

In Spring 1997 and again in Spring 1998, Kaye Edwards and I co-taught the single required course for all Feminist and Gender Studies concentrators at Bryn Mawr and Haverford Colleges, a long-established but ever-more-ambitious junior-level seminar entitled "Interdisciplinary Perspectives in Gender." Kaye and I enjoyed the time we spent together, sifting through the vast range of material we felt obliged to cover in "defining" the contemporary field(s) of gender studies and shaping it into what we hoped would be manageable form for the wide range of students we expected to take the course.

In an attempt to give a certain coherence to the reading list, we selected an organizing theme—"Knowing the Body"—and arranged the material in seven stages, beginning with what the students knew experientially and (we thought) would be willing and able to speak comfortably about, then moving sequentially into material which we expected to be less well known to and increasingly problematic for them. We began with a section called "Our Bodies Experienced," with readings and films on menstruation, being breasted, body shape, sexual experience, and the disabled and dying body. The second section, "Bodies of Evidence/Bodies of Knowledge," raised questions about the authority of experiential knowledge and focused on a wide range of issues concerning epistemology, interdisciplinarity, and pedagogy. The third section questioned the naturalness of "Body Form" by examining the issues of intersex and transgender. The fourth section of the course, "Body Talk/Body Language," gave attention to Madonna, the pornography debates, and various forms of *l'écriture féminine;* the fifth, "The Body in Law," examined the work of Patricia Williams, considered the Thomas-Hill debates, and a range of legal questions: those having to do with sexual violence, contraceptive technology and reproductive rights. In the sixth section of the course, "The Body Politic," we turned our attention to questions of global feminism, asking about our political, economic and ethical relationship with and under-standing of women in other parts of the world. We discussed essays on tourism, garment factories, domestic servants, international migrants, female genital surgeries, terrorism, and questions of diet, such as those raised by breastfeeding amidst the AIDS epidemic and the practice of "feminist vegetarianism."

We also invited Linda Caruso-Haviland, a colleague who directs the dance program at Bryn Mawr, to initiate a number of our class sessions. Introducing herself to the students as an artist, a dancer, and a woman who found herself "suspect as a knower" in our intellectual community, Linda returned periodically throughout the semester to direct us in a series of exercises in movement designed to foreground our embodiness as an aspect of our knowing. In what ways does the body serve as a source of knowledge? What difference does it make if we experience knowing as an embodied process, if we acknowledge that we are embodied thinkers? Is it necessary—is it possible—to give voice to such embodiment? What form, what value, what limits might such expression have?

We undertook this challenging project—showcasing the wide range of questions considered in the varied field of gender studies, featuring the multiple ways in which disciplines as disparate as biology and dance addressed such questions—with students who ran the gamut from those just beginning to realize that gender might be a productive lens for asking questions about the world to those with much more sophisticated theoretical understandings. Given the range of both the students and the work we were attending to, our encounters with each of the texts were inevitably piecemeal. We became conscious before the first week of classes ended that our students felt hurried through the expanse of topics and the multiple perspectives on each.

Trying to organize and control such an unwieldy project, Kaye and I spent lots of thought and energy structuring each individual class period. A common form, for example, included what Kaye termed—and I gleefully embraced as—an "exponential conversation." We would pose a question and break the class into pairs or triads to discuss it; after ten or fifteen minutes, we would ask them to re-combine into groups of four or six as we posed another question; quarter of an hour later came yet another, larger re-combination and another follow-up question. Finally the group as a whole wrestled with a yet larger question. Although a number of students appreciated the opportunities to speak afforded by small group work, there was also considerable resistance to our structure, both from students who wanted more help in moving through the stages of the conversation and—more vociferously—from those who wanted less, who objected to the constant moving-on, the steady professorial manipulation: before they felt they had finished with one question, we were nudging them on to the next.

During the semester, as Abby reports, one of the metaphors we used to describe our teaching was that of hostesses at a dinner party. Kaye and I saw ourselves as and took great delight in doing almost all the "cooking," providing, preparing and serving the "food." We asked of our students that they be good guests: arriving in joyful anticipation and joyfully "chewing over" what we had prepared for their pleasure and instruction. But ofttimes they did not appreciate our hospitality. Abby's pronounced critique of our management of classroom interactions explicitly uses the metaphor of the class as dinner party in which we took such delight to describe the failure of the hostesses. Why, she asks, did Kaye and I not "value every individual voice"? Why did we "permit" some women to dominate our class discussion? Why did we "acknowledge and accept" their domination? Why did we "allow" the "silent, voiceless majority" to act as the audience for others? Worse, when she called our attention to the imbalance, why did Abby experience our intervention—our encouraging the silent to speak—not as our welcoming her contribution to class but rather as being "co-opted," "selective," "excluding"?

Abby critiques our structuring of the classroom as insistent yet ineffectual. From her report, I can see now how such structuring produced resentment, because it implied that our students were themselves unable to formulate the structures they needed. Diane Brunner has written similarly about the ways in which supervisors' lesson plans—what she calls "recipes"—perpetuate dependency, suggest a lack of "confidence in teachers' capabilities to make good decisions" (46, 52). Professors' unrelenting structuring suggests our lack of trust that the students in our classes, with their variety of interests and concerns, can productively find their own ways through a multiplicity of material. Kaye and I certainly saw it as our responsibility to guide our students and often did so by dictating the direction and the pace of their classroom conversation. Our concern, in Foucault's terms, was with forms of "government": "the way in which the conduct of individuals or groups might be directed...to structure the possible field of action" (Gore, *The Struggle for Pedagogies* 52).

I have long seen my role in my classes as establishing such a structure. As Abby observes, when one of my earlier students withdrew from a class (and the college) in profound dissatisfaction with our classroom conversations, I characterized my emotional state not in terms of the kind of food we had been sharing or the ways we had been preparing it but by calling attention to the construction I had designed for those conversations to take place. I repeatedly told colleagues that I had tried to build in my classroom "a table large and steady enough for everyone to sit around" and was troubled by my failure to do so. I held myself accountable for my inability to construct a framework that would have enabled all of us to continue talking with one another.

My operative metaphor at the time was less that of party hostess than that of a role that carries decidedly different marks of class and gender but assumes many of the same responsibilities. It is well described in Ann Stanton's metaphor for teaching:

> a construction site where the teacher, surrounded by apprentices, is simultaneously architect, general contractor, and supervisor and where a variety of tools are required, numerous action sequences must be coordinated vis-à-vis the design, and the emerging structure is continually tested for soundness. What are those tools and action sequences? What are design features? How does the structure hold up? (41)

Prodded by Abby's critique, and by the similar work of postmodern pedagogical theorists, I am questioning now the kind and even the amount of attention I have been paying to the structuring of conversations in my classrooms. Like Abby, Jennifer Gore shows how critical feminist pedagogies can operate as "regimes of truth" that "have dominating effects" (xii). Gore's book, *The Struggle for Pedagogies*, focuses on the difficulty of throwing off the regulative aspects of pedagogy. Jane Gallop's collection on pedagogical impersonation similarly examines the cultural placement and managerial functions of our personal relations with our students (161–162). From the instruction of such texts and far more pointed instruction of my own students, I am belatedly coming to understand a certain profound dynamic: the more scrupulously I structure my classroom, the more insistently resistance will be produced. As Geoff Harpham glosses Foucault, such a reaction is internal to the relation:

> Where there is power, there is resistance...this resistance is never in a position of exteriority in relation to power...Resisted power is...multiple, relational and unstable...in its functioning...Resistance...is the site and condition of power...Power-resistance is...a figure of relation. (*The Ascetic Imperative* 231)

Reflective teachers have long acknowledged this relation and the level of its intensity between adult teachers and their adolescent students. Mary Rose O'Reilley focuses on the healthy psychology of students' needs for resistance: "The natural work of young people is to subvert and challenge the authority of teacher and parent, no matter how 'enlightened.' This is perhaps their primary learning experience. They are, in some strategic sense, the opposition" (*The Peaceable Classroom* 68).

Drawing on Hebdige's study of adolescent subculture, Patti Lather gives a similar account of student dislike of "being understood" by their elders and asks whether teachers' attempts to overcome such resistance are appropriate:

> "'You really hate an adult to understand you. That's the only thing you've got over them, the fact that you can mystify and worry them.' Contemporary youth have cause to be wary of giving up their

anonymity, of making their private and lived voices the object of public and pedagogical scrutiny." To what extent is the pedagogy we construct in the name of liberation intrusive, invasive, pressured? (143)

To what extent is such a pedagogy even possible? Guided by such observations, I now understand Abby's reticence to speak in our class as a complex enactment of her resistance to our directed discussions, what Magda Lewis describes as "a conscious decision to refrain from the discussion as a form of resistance to being silenced" (Lewis and Simon 463).

In her essay, Abby describes her silence as both countenanced by her teachers, who established the structure within which speaking and silencing occurred, and imposed on her by her classmates, whom she characterizes as twice "comfortable," even "complacent" about their dominant speaking roles. But Abby was not really bound, as she complains she was, by the disciplinary action of the talking circle. Rather, she refused to be disciplined into the discourse designed by her professors and enacted by her group of peers. In her resistance, she exercised power in the complex unstable play of relations that was our classroom. Her silence—even more, her sighs of frustration—signaled less what Orner's image of the panopticon implies, the fearful silence of being judged by a circle of peers, all of whom have internalized the academic expectations of their professors, than an impatience with the direction of our discussion. Tense and twisting, sighing loudly in her seat, Abby brought her own complacencies into our classroom.

Abby, next semester

I'm back from senior seminar, an intense class of only eight very bright students. And I didn't speak again this week. I talked to the professor casually after class and I hung out with some of the students afterwards: we talked and laughed at a local bar, and they asked me why I don't talk in class. And after blaming my silence in Anne's class on a failure of the "ethic of care," on the panopticon, on anything and everyone I could, I still don't have an explanation. I'm quiet in big classes and little classes, feminist classrooms and more traditional classrooms. I don't walk out of any of my classes seething this semester, but I clearly haven't come to voice either. But as I said before, I'm not really sure I believe that anyone comes to voice in a sustained way anyhow.

But what I want to look at more carefully is the looking relations that take place in classrooms. Anne and I have described Foucauldian disciplinary power and how the model of the panopticon might play out in the classroom as the authority of the talking circle. Most obviously, there is no center watch tower in the classroom; rather, each subject is constituted by the multiple gaze of the other subjects in the classroom. Anne has written about her gaze on me, about her recognizing my displeasure with the class: "Tense and twisting, sighing loudly in her seat, Abby brought her own complacencies into our classroom." I was surprised that Anne noticed. While I knew that she was aware of the absence of my voice, I didn't realize that she saw me being silent. I had been aware of my physical discomfort in the classroom, my watching the clock and occasionally of my sighs, but I hadn't been aware of their effect in the classroom, that I was being watched and heard by up to thirty other people. Anne's gaze apprehended me, reading my silence as complacent.

It seems to me that we need to focus not so much on silence, but rather on speech as part of this parasubjective matrix in which we are constituted by multiple gazes. We speak, twist and sigh under the gaze of others in the classroom. As Foucault wrote in *History of Sexuality*,

> Silence itself—the things one declines to say, or is forbidden to name, the discretion that is required between different speakers—is less the absolute limit of discourse, the other side from which it is separated by a strict boundary, than an element that functions alongside the things said, with them and in relation to them within overall strategies. There is no binary division to be made between what one says and what one does not say; we must try to determine the different ways of not saying such things, how those who can and those who cannot speak of them are distributed, which type of discourse is authorized, or which form of discretion is required in either case. There is not one but many silences, and they are an integral part of the strategies that underlie and permeate discourses. (27)

Anne

Abby is helping me see the inadequacy of the language of surveillance, of the unidirectional activity of the panopticon for describing the ambivalent, complex interplay in classrooms such as ours, which are composed as much of the conversational and interactive dynamic of silence and sound as of looking and being seen. Feminist pedagogical alternatives that express esteem and care also now seem insufficient to me for tracing the complex force fields that are my classes.

In *Foucault: A Critical Reader*, Martin Jay calls attention to the anti-visual dimension of Foucault's discourse. In his interrogation of the privileged role Western philosophy has granted to sight as the most trustworthy of the senses, Foucault emphasized its problematics: he examined the hostile scrutiny of the scientific gaze, the sinister ocular centrism of panopticism, the normalizing gaze of the technology of power. The complicated sensation of being the target of the gaze invokes the prophylactic power of surveillance: the object internalizes the external look, becomes self-regulating, appropriates to the self the surveillance of the panoptic machine.

Jay ends his essay by tracing alternative forms of seeing. He describes, for example, the "optic of astonishment," laying out the possibility of the "mutual glance"—reciprocal, intersubjective, communicative—a kind of regard that is caring, esteeming, that delights in the visual, rather than fears being seen (195). Feminist theorists are well known for their exploration of such interactive processes. Perhaps most useful for our study here is the work of those who have explored alternative forms that focus not on enhancing the mutuality of sight—an operation which would call attention back to the needs of the self—but rather on the decided concentration on the other, which involves a turning away from one's own concerns.

Marilyn Frye, for instance, develops a contrast between the arrogant and the loving eye, which "knows the independence of the other" and must "look and listen and check and question." Sally McFague cites Frye in her articulation of the practice of "attention epistemology," "the kind of knowledge that comes from paying close attention to something other than oneself...

listening...to the other, in itself, for itself" (49–52). In their descriptions of careful, attentive seeing, both Frye and McFague use the word "listening." The alternative practices of seeing they describe exercise not the sound of one's own voice but a sense of audition. As they conceptualize and practice sight, it is incomplete without careful hearing.

Much contemporary feminist pedagogy enacts such a model and adds to the qualities of attentive listening the necessity of caring response. Jane Tompkins is probably the best-known English professor to describe and attempt to revise what she calls the primary method of classroom practice in the United States, "the performance model":

> I had finally realized that what I was actually concerned with and focused on most of the time were three things: 1) to show the students how smart I was, b) to show them how knowledgeable I was, and c) to show them how well-prepared I was for class. I had been putting on a performance whose true goal was not to help the students learn but to perform before them in such a way that they would have a good opinion of me. I think that this essentially, and more than anything else, is what we teach our students: how to perform within an institutional academic setting in such a way that they will be thought highly of by their colleagues and instructors. ("Pedagogy of the Distressed" 654)

In this performance model of classroom work, Tompkins argues, "we came to be split into two parts: the real backstage self who didn't know anything and the performing self who got others to believe in its expertise and accomplishments" (654–655). Tompkins's solution for that dilemma, like that of many feminist educators, involved the attempt to replace her own interests with those of her students, to move backstage center:

> I wanted to get "out there" and "in here" together. To forge a connection between what we were talking about in class and what went on in the lives of the individual members...I can never fool myself into believing that what I have to say is ultimately more important to the students than what they think and feel. I know now that each student is a walking field of energy teeming with agendas...I can conduct my classes so as to tap into that energy field. (658–659)

Tompkins's giving over the role of performer for that of audience constituted an invitation to her students to reverse those roles. And yet the "performance mentality" still, unyieldingly, structured her classroom—or at least her description of it—even after she removed herself "from center stage" (660):

> When I embarked on my experiments in teaching, I thought I was putting the performance mentality behind me by putting students at the center of things. But now I see that the experiment itself became my performance. Only now my success or failure depended on the performance of the students. (*Life* 162–163)

Underlying the account of the roles played in Tompkins' class as well as in my own are two settled binaries. First is the notion that each member of the class can fulfill only one part at a time: whoever is not performing constitutes the audience for the spectacle, which operates in one direction only as the audience receives what the actors project. A more fundamental binary undergirds the unidirectional model of the first, an assumption which the art critic Craig Owens identifies as the traditional theatrical

> structure of representation...the imitation, rather than the immediate presentation, of action [which] posits a fundamental dualism at the heart of the theater...that rift...between the tangible physical presence of the performer and that absence which is necessarily implicated in any concept of imitation...Thus what is represented is always an "elsewhere"...while the performer is...a presence...we always regard him...as a representative for something else—the actor as perpetual stand-in. (3)

Tompkins conceived of her students as actors "standing in" for selves who are "really" situated elsewhere and of her classroom as a space in which she invited them to perform the concerns which "really" motivate them outside of it. The same binary underlay Kaye's and my endless inventions to get our students to "represent themselves" in our classroom; our multiple invitations were intended to provoke sustained performance from them. We judged our success as teachers—as often, we judged our failure—

by our students' exhibitions and, like Tompkins, were disappointed to find them not always as engaged as we wished.

I will recount here only one, but perhaps the most revealing, of such scripts: the class Abby later described to me, finely punning, as a "spectacular failure." While we were teaching "Knowing the Body," Kaye and I both enrolled in a tri-college faculty seminar on the politics and poetics of corporeality, entitled "Engaging Bodies." Led by Anne Cooper Albright, who is trained both in philosophy and performance studies, the seminar was designed to investigate the relationship of cross-disciplinary dialogue to experienced bodiedness. We were attempting both to theorize our "body work" and to expand our understanding of intellectual work to encompass bodily pleasure.

One evening, in response to our accounts of the resistant dynamics of our gender studies classroom, Anne Albright suggested to the faculty group that one reason it feels so risky to speak in a classroom—especially to speak about issues of political correctness and incorrectness—is because we never know what others are thinking: we speak into a great silent circle, without any gestures of support or opposition. She hypothesized that gesturing as we spoke, or even more as we listened, might address and calm such fears.

Kaye and I experimented with the use of such gesturing at the first opportunity—in our next class period. We began by asking our colleague in dance, Linda Haviland, to open the class with a series of exercises. In the past, whenever Linda had initiated the class with movement, we had afterwards settled in to talk in the same old ways, fixing ourselves, as one student said, "like ladies who can't move, in the corsets of our chairs." There was little, if any, carryover from the movement exercises to the discussion.

This day, however, we invited our students and ourselves to keep on moving as we talked, to be more expressive with our bodies as we spoke. We conducted this class, as all others, in words, but we attempted to add another layer, asking the students—if they were talking—to express what they were saying in gestures as well as words and—if they were not—to express in gestures what they were thinking. We also asked the students to move around: if they agreed with what someone was saying, to move over to her; if they disagreed, to move away; if they were ambivalent (the response of most of us, most of the time), to find some position to say so with their bodies—to try, throughout the discussion, to use gestures to figure their thinking.

Some of the students already did this occasionally but we tried, that day, to institute gesturing as a general principle of articulation, a means of "improved communication." I rather enjoyed the exercise, which seemed to me to bring a dimension of play and fun into our often-earnest discussion. A few students— who were involved in campus theater—also entered gamely into the experiment, but eventually, Megan Munson asked that we stop, saying that the movements were "too distracting," that the gestures made it hard for her to attend to what her classmates were saying. After the semester ended, I got a letter from another student, Kim Newman, musing, "you prefer to speak, in a way to be center stage (just consider the class where we were supposed to enact what we felt). I prefer to listen...which is what I do in class. Sit back and analyze what I hear."

Such failed pedagogical interventions, I now can see, relied on modernist theatrical notions that work poorly as models for our classroom discussions. Our efforts to attain what Judith Butler calls "an approximation of realness" (*Bodies* 129) by getting our students to "act out" in class what they "really" thought and felt constituted particularly subtle versions of the "indignity of representation":

> there is a celebrated passage in the *Eighteenth Brumaire* in which Marx...concludes with the famous remark, "They cannot represent themselves, they must be represented"...his self-appointed task was to represent the interests of those whom he presumed to be incapable of representing themselves...Here, Marx ...appropriates for himself the right to speak on behalf of others, setting himself up as their consciences,—indeed, as consciousness itself. But in order to occupy this position, he must first deny them (self-)consciousness, the ability to represent themselves..."[Foucault was the first] to teach us something absolutely fundamental: the indignity of speaking for others"...It is precisely in being represented by the dominant culture that [marginalized] groups have been rendered absences within it...the activity of representation itself...by denying them speech,

consciousness, the ability to represent themselves, stands indicted as the primary agent of their domination. (Owens 261–262)

Owens doesn't articulate the further turn of the screw enacted in our class: that of our insisting that students "represent themselves" in certain forms, gestures, and language. But his analysis does suggest that the modernist conception of performance as the representation of an absence which is "always an elsewhere" (3) is no more adequate and no more ethical than either panoptic surveillance or attention epistemology for describing the complex interactions which take place in our classrooms.

The operating conception in Abby's essay—the presumed model that she charges us with deviating from—is that of competition for limited airtime, a democratic arrangement of equal time for each voice. Abby complains that her classmates, who were intent on articulating their own perceptions, did not attend to and did not make space for her own. But not all the quiet students in our gender class were envious of those who spoke, not all felt "trampled on" in the way that Abby describes. Some of them argued, conversely, for the right to be—even the virtue of being—silent. Amanda Moon, for instance, mused in an e-mail message,

> Sitting in class the other day, I wondered where was our space for silence, for listening to one another and not just worrying about needing to say something that contributes to class learning…I feel that listening can also contribute to class learning. If you say something aloud it is nice to have listeners who are actually listening. If all of the students in the class were constantly competing to be able to speak, no one would be listening to each other and no real dialogues would occur. I have come to realize after four years of college that saying something just for the sake of having spoken is often more detrimental to learning than saying nothing at all. I want a space in this class to be accepted for listening to others speak and not to feel judged…that I haven't said enough. When I have something to say, I will say it; not every time will it be deep and meaningful, but possibly the chances are higher if I am only speaking when moved to do so…I have contributed through my listening, and if this is not enough I will suffer the consequences.

Amanda's testimony to the value of careful listening is simultaneously, and strikingly, also a declaration of the felt violence of being forced to speak and of the expectation of being punished (with a lower grade) for her failure to do so. The anticipated suffering, with which the report of her resistance ends, gestures at the ongoing classroom project that Abby describes: "the parasubjective matrix in which we are constituted by multiple gazes." Postmodern performance theorists such as Butler have studied this process extensively: the intricate, uncertain ways in which we are socially constituted in our interactions with others. Seen and heard by others—perhaps especially when students and teachers are attentively, carefully, respectfully seen and heard by one another—we participate in the formation of one another as subjects, both responsive and resistant to classroom expectations.

I now hear the silences of both Abby and Amanda as complicated—but productive—responses to their interpellation as students in our classroom. My understanding of their resistances, of their "refusal to be disciplined," as profoundly positive engagements with the work of the class derives largely from Butler's work. In *Bodies That Matter*, Butler investigates the ways in which we confound the "disciplining intention" of others' designs upon us:

> this juncture of discursive demands is something like a "crossroads" ...the subject...is always the nexus...of cultural collision, in which the demand...cannot be summarily refused, but neither...followed in strict obedience...the space of this ambivalence... opens up the possibility of a reworking of the very terms by which subjectivation proceeds—and fails to proceed. (122, 124)

When engaged students like Abby and Amanda fall silent in a feminist classroom at Bryn Mawr, such an ongoing process—what Butler calls a "ritualized practice"—seems to me to be at work: our discussions are insistently bound by, yet as insistently unbinding and reconfiguring, multiple conventions, which we perform as if they are unscripted and spontaneous (*Excitable Speech* 51).

Such language—which is drawn from that of contemporary performance studies, rather than from modernist theatrical conventions—helps me better understand some of the complexities in my classroom engagements. In their study of performativity, for instance, Andrew Parker and Eve Sedgwick observe that "identities are constructed iteratively through complex citational processes...Differing crucially...from a more familiar...interrogation of the gaze, this interrogation of the space of reception involves [multiple] contradictions and discontinuities" (2, 7). Particularly productive for an analysis of resistances like those of Abby and Amanda may be the attention Parker and Sedgwick give to the "fascinating and powerful class of negative performatives—disavowal, renunciation, repudiation, 'count me out'" (9). Parker and Sedgwick's examination of "the silence of witness," "the bare, negative, potent but undiscretionary speech act of our physical presence...that ratifies and recruits" (10–11), suggests to me, for instance, the degree to which our classroom is "constituted as a spectacle that denies its audience the ability either to look away from it or equally to intervene in it" (11).

Postmodern performance theory gives me useful ways of re-considering spectacles such as the one that occurred when, on the first day of class, a former student greeted me with a kiss on the cheek. In doing so, she asserted a prior relationship, claimed me publicly as a friend—a construction that relied on the gaze of the whole class as verification. But the space in which she "performed" and in which they "attended" is far more complicated than such language suggests. How did that kiss play out for the others in the class? Did they feel left out? Put off? Invited into a similar relationship with their teacher? Just what was the relationship figured by that kiss?

Such interactions in our feminist classrooms might be productively re-imagined as ongoing explorations that rely less on "spectatorship" and "surveillance," "theater" and "representation" than on the reciprocal dynamics of sight and its return, of sound and silence, laced with the interactive work we perform with our moving bodies. In the work of contemporary performance theory, I find alternative understandings of the exercise of professorial authority and of student reaction, which both acknowledge our unending performance in the classroom and convince me that I need not, indeed cannot, control it as insistently as I have tried to do in the past.

In acknowledging the limits of my ability to control "what happens" in my classes, I am also following some of the feminist theoretical revision of Nel Noddings' work on the ethic of care, in particular that of Sarah Hoagland, who questions the appropriateness of acting on behalf of someone else (249, 254), and that of Sharon Welch, who similarly problematizes the deep-seated ethic of control that underlies "responsible" action for the European-American middle class (1, 3).

Following Welch's invitation to a "different calculus of risk" (6), I want to return now to *The Dinner Party*, which Abby used so strikingly to figure her critique of our class and re-consider its usefulness as an image of our engagement. In her meditation on the role of the women on the *Heritage Floor*, whose position she found analogous to her own silence in the classroom, Abby called attention to the practices of exclusion embedded in Chicago's installation: "They are the foundation," she said, "inscribed on the floor, hungry and walked upon." Numerous contemporary feminist critics have similarly faulted Chicago for being "driven by the desire for mastery and achievement" (Meyer 71) and failing "to fulfill the collaborative goals of 1970s feminist theory" (Jones 108).

Revisiting *The Dinner Party*, I am, of course, acutely conscious of the relation between the women at the table and those on the floor: the latter figure for me as the many women who are not themselves engaged in but well may be the subject of our classroom discussions. I notice the multiple, contradictory roles played by the women at the table, as by the students Abby described: "those few who speak in class, those who own the class, to whom the class really belongs." Such an image of pure and simple "possession" fails to describe either the contradictions of Chicago's exhibition or the unstable interplay of our classroom dynamics.

Chicago's initial conception of a series of painted plates evoked the historical silencing of women: "I thought images on plates would convey the fact that the women I planned to represent had been swallowed up and obscured by history" (8).

She was attracted to the medium of china painting as "a perfect metaphor for women's domesticated and trivialized circumstances" (11). Under the early working title of "Twenty-Five Women Who Were Eaten Alive," she conceived of her project as symbolizing the ways in which "women's achievements had been left out of history and the records of their lives had apparently disappeared":

> I began to think about the piece as a reinterpretation of the Last Supper from the point of view of women, who, throughout history, had prepared the meals and set the table. In my "Last Supper," however, the women would be the honored guests. Their representation in the form of plates set on the table would express the way women had been confined, and the piece would thus reflect both women's achievements and their oppression. (11)

That double impulse played out as the project developed. The plates became increasingly three-dimensional, to suggest that women had become, in time, "increasingly active" in their efforts "to escape from the plate" (13–14). Chicago came to describe the women represented by the plates not as the food but as the dinner guests: "I invited them to dinner, so to speak—in order that we might hear what they have to say" (52).

A profound contradiction is embedded in Chicago's installation as in our classrooms. The women who sit at the table have been invited to "to dinner." To eat what? Themselves? Products produced by other women? They are themselves represented by such products. If they have been invited "to speak," what do they say? Is their eating—and speaking—performative? Is their performance what is being eaten? By us, who, as spectators, consume this exhibition?

The multiple possible answers to these questions, the sheer *unendingness* of such questions, make Chicago's exhibition still useful to me as a metaphor for understanding what happens in my classroom. I now understand her project, however, not as a modernist exhibition of women "frozen" in their historical moments but rather in the postmodern sense that Laura Meyer evokes when she traces the collaborative work that went into the making of *The Dinner Party*. An important aspect of contemporary performance work, Meyer implies, is that it is productive of further performance. *The Dinner Party*

> took on the quality of a performance piece, a quality that was highlighted by Suzanne Lacy's gift to Chicago on the eve of its San Francisco Opening—the twenty-four-hour *International Dinner Party*, in which women around the world gathered to honor the women of their choice, sending telegrams to Lacy, who marked the celebrations with lighted pins on a map of the world at the San Francisco Museum of Modern Art. (68)

Elin Diamond suggests that what is particularly unending in contemporary performance art is the discomfort produced by the display. Diamond begins her essay on "The Shudder of Catharsis in Twentieth-Century Performance" by correcting Lacan's conception of the dialectic of the eye and the gaze—"the subject I/eye always manipulated in field of vision that precedes her, bound up with look of the Other." Calling attention to the disjunction, the "disturbing oscillation" between seeing and feeling (153), Diamond describes a form of postmodern performance that leaves "no space for representation": Karen Finley's "acts of total expenditure," Diamond suggests, refuse the separation of performance and "the true-real." "Though at some point the performance will end, what is suggested is shuddering without end: permanent catharsis" (165–166).

I confess that I began this project with the hope that the shuddering in and over my classroom *might* end. I was troubled by the anger which surfaces in an early paragraph of Abby's essay, is ascribed by her to other "sullen," "fierce," "furious" students in its center and is finally re-invoked as celebratory but quite aimless in its finale: "Anger is challenging and necessary," "should be felt and acknowledged," gives "a sense of being," "an awareness of worth. It is a lovely surging." I doubt it felt lovely to Abby as—trying to get out of that essay—she wrote that line. It sure did not feel lovely to me as I read it—and I invited Abby to collaborate with me in this chapter, in hopes of assuaging that anger.

I had larger aims as well. I expected that Abby would find ways to intervene more productively in such spaces in the future, and that I would find the means of setting up classroom spaces more generative for students as hungry and angry as Abby was the semester she studied with me and continued to be thereafter.

Abby, two semesters later

I'm a T.A. for a class. Two male students and the male professor talked the whole time in class today. The male professor seemed stuck refereeing an increasingly unrelated and stultifying conversation. Unfortunately, he ended up ignoring one whole side of the room. On that side were most of the women, all of them silent. As the T.A., I had the authority to intervene, even to silence if I'd wanted. But I sat there, trying to make eye contact with the prof, feeling frustrated that I hadn't made any progress myself. I didn't leap in when the overconfident boy started talking about the AARP in a class that was supposed to be about queer politics. What should I do when people start talking to one another, and I'm not interested, and I don't know how to get them to stop? I need to learn, because that kind of intellectual masturbation isn't useful for anyone but those boys. That's how I felt last year, and that is how I felt today; though it might be gendered differently, I think it's the same phenomenon.

That's why I need a prescription, a frustrating way to break up the frustrating pattern of passionate silence. Because something that being a t.a. has taught me is that I know things, that I have something to say, that I like talking to people about ideas and learning together. But I can't stand it when all the women in the room are checking their watches while two boys (seemingly) unself-consciously have a conversation between themselves when we're all supposed to know better by now. I'm clinging to the idea that there's something better than angrily watching them perform. If I'm capable of intervening, then I need to know how to do so. If I sit in frustration, with the thought that I can do something, that there is something I know that I'm unable to articulate that could maybe make this better, then I want to learn how to articulate it.

Anne

I had hoped that re-examining our experiences in the classroom might enable Abby and me to figure out just what—not only in our own psychology and educational histories but in the structure and organization of the class, of the program, of the college, of the U.S. educational program largely conceived— contributed to her anger. I trusted that we might move beyond acknowledging and celebrating that anger, to re-figuring the structure that induced it. Abby's description of her experience as a teaching assistant confirms that re-working classroom structures can be enabling for a student: being a t.a. has "taught" her, for instance, that she "know things," that she "has something to say."

I cannot answer, however, Abby's call for a "prescription," a "script" that will enable her to intervene when the classroom conversation seems to go astray. In Diamond's description of Finley's performance I find an alternative model—or at least a new metaphor—for what might happen in our classes. The story Abby and I have re-traced here is not one in which anger is purged—nor, I've come to realize, is such catharsis possible. In her essay and her postscripts, Abby requests more disciplinary action. She wishes that her classmates would discipline themselves, be guided by the ethics of responsiveness to one another's needs, and—when they fail to do so—complains that her professors (and later, she herself, as t.a.) "allow" a few students to dominate the discussion. But I understand now that fulfilling Abby's request for more definitive structure would simply—well, not so simply—produce additional resistance, new forms of frustration and anger.

Abby

And now I realize the absurdity of looking for a script to control the more dominant (often more charismatic or verbally confident) students in my classrooms. This idea seems to pre-suppose an omnipotent professor who possesses all the answers and control. Cramming students with their different expectations and desires into a room is a volatile mix, one that a professor can't be expected transparently to comprehend. If I can't know how to productively intervene as a T.A., then I can't expect my professors to know the way to satisfy everyone's desires.

Anne

Owens's description of postmodern art works well as a description of our narrative: it is one of "contingency, insufficiency, lack of transcendence. It tells of a desire that must be perpetually frustrated, an ambition that must be perpetually deferred" (85). In acknowledging now the unending production of resistance and anger in the classroom, we also celebrate, however, the unendingness of the desire that feeds it.

The structure of the classroom as we have experienced and interpreted it involves no release. But it is precisely and not at all paradoxically the absence of fulfillment, that continual hunger, which brings me—and I think, many of my colleagues and students—repeatedly and longingly back into the classroom. As Geoff Harpham, still following Foucault, observes, "resistances are the points of pleasurable friction, of painful opposition...'what gives "power" its power' is its complicity with desire.'" Tracing an "ambivalent ambition to remain within the situation of temptation/resistance," Harpham suggests that one revealing way to approach one's object of study "is by asking what account of desire it presupposes, what temptations it foresees, and how it proposes to resist them" (*The Ascetic Imperative* 264, 231–232, 245).

The structure of the classroom induces unending resistance, which is a mark of our unending desire. But it is also that hunger which opens us to be fed. Our anger, our dissatisfaction, our emptiness, is the space in which we receive what we most need, as Audre Lorde says in "For Each of You":

> When you are hungry
> learn to eat
> whatever sustains you...
> everything can be used...
> If you do not learn to hate
> you will never be lonely
> enough
> to love easily

Windows. Thomas Hall. Bryn Mawr College.
Photograph by Carlos Garcia. 2001.

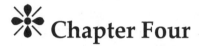 **Chapter Four**

"Silence Is So Windowful":
Class as Antechamber

Love silence even in the mind; for thoughts are to that, as
words to the body, troublesome; much speaking, as much
thinking, spends, and in many thoughts, as well as words,
there is sin. True silence is…nourishment and refreshment.
It is a great virtue; it covers folly, keeps secrets, avoids
disputes, and prevents sin.
                    William Penn, *Advice to His Children*

You can listen to silence…and learn from it. It has a quality
and a dimension all its own…a strange, beautiful text-
ure…Sometimes it cries, and you can hear the pain of the
world in it…And it is important to know of pain. It des-
troys our self-pride, our arrogance, our indifference toward
others. It makes us aware of how frail and tiny we are.
                    Chaim Potok, *The Chosen* (262, 278)

I have been a Quaker for nearly fifteen years, an academic for over
twenty, and am still struggling with what often seems to me an
incongruity (an incompatibility? an irrationality? certainly a
marked tension) between the articulate speech which academic
work values and the silence of Quaker worship, that reminds me
so often of the miseries and mysteries of life better apprehended
when we refrain from speech. I want to trace here some of the
complexities of this inter-relationship by mulling over a few
stories of the silences that pervaded my two-year shared class-

room experiment with Kaye Edwards, a biologist who teaches at Haverford College. It seems to me now that I made a mistake in our course, one I can learn from and try to correct each time I return to the classroom: a failure to trust my Quaker knowledge of the expressive and exploratory powers of silence. Following Elizabeth Ellsworth's query, I investigate such possibilities here:

> What kind of educational project would redefine the silence of the unknowable, freeing it from…"Absence, Lack, and Fear," and make of that silence "a language of its own that changes the nature and direction of speech itself?" (113)

Kaye and I first found one another not at Haverford, where she teaches, or at Bryn Mawr, where I do, but on the deck at Radnor Friends' Meeting. Picking up our kids after worship, we soon discovered that we were mothers with children of overlapping ages, that we lived in the same town, and that we both taught in the bi-co (the term used by Haverford and Bryn Mawr Colleges to name their collaborative association). Eventually, we confided to one another that our positions within our institutions were unusual, that we were currently negotiating new arrangements with our colleagues and administrators. While Kaye was downsizing, relocating from a tenure-track position in the Haverford Biology Department to a part-time appointment in General Programs, I was moving on a very gradual upward trajectory, teaching more than I had in the past, turning a part-time job in the Bryn Mawr English Department into a slow-track career. As our paths crossed, we settled in very similar positions and found a location in the same alternative space: the bi-college program of Feminist and Gender Studies, a collegial group of people from a wide variety of departments and both colleges, interested in the questions raised by looking at gender as a category of analysis. Eventually, we arranged to co-teach the core course of the program, a junior-level seminar called "Interdisciplinary Perspectives on Gender: Knowing the Body."

Our friendship had begun in a spiritual context and, appropriately, the first meeting to plan our new course took place in a spiritual setting. During Kaye's sabbatical, she had begun a tradition of monthly two-day sojourns at Pendle Hill, the Quaker Study Center in Wallingford, Pennsylvania, a place where she could braid together her spiritual and academic lives. She suggested that we begin our course planning there. On a warm June day, we sat on the hill outside the Barn and talked about how to integrate biology and literary analysis in the teaching of feminist and gender studies. After our first session at Pendle Hill, we worked interdependently not only across disciplines but across state borders. We next met over the 4th of July, surrounded by both our families at my farm in Virginia.

While our husbands and children fished, we did stretching exercises on the front porch of the farm house and began crafting a syllabus, reading list, and set of requirements. Back on campus in the fall, we organized our meetings around Kaye's appetite and my exercise schedule. Monthly, then weekly, eventually—once class began in the spring semester—every Monday and Wednesday morning, we met over breakfast to discuss the shape of the course. At the end of the semester, we came full circle, returning to Pendle Hill to attend a weekend conference on spiritual friendship.

Kaye and I brought into our interdisciplinary teaching a shared sense of institutional marginality but also many shared intellectual interests, a shared educational mission and focus and a shared theology: a belief in that of God in everyone, in our students, in each other. We also brought differences in training, in background, in pacing. What enabled us to negotiate such differences were spiritual things: patience, trust, friendship, a willingness to listen, to be corrected. But that process was far from a simple one, as a simple example will show.

For several years, Kaye had initiated each of her own classes with a period of silence, a means of gathering herself and her students into the space of the classroom and the work which lay before them that hour. She suggested that we also begin our shared classes in this way. It was easy for me to assent to her request the first year we taught together in the Haverford College science building; it was more difficult for me to do so the second year when we taught in the administration building at Bryn Mawr. I was leery of that silence, largely because I saw it as a transgression against the operative paradigm of my workplace. As Helen Horowitz has shown, the Quaker founders of Bryn Mawr College had envisoned it as a "female copy" of Haverford, a place where conservative Friends could send their daughters (106, 111). Its second president, M. Carey Thomas, whose vision really defined the college as it exists today, was raised as an orthodox Friend and used her Quaker connections to secure her position there (113). But Thomas soon transfigured "what began as a Quaker college for women into a secular and cosmopolitan institution," one that turned decisively away from "adherence to Quaker traditions" (116–117). Thomas saw Friends as obstacles to her ideal of Bryn Mawr: a place where women could succeed at the kind of rigorous academic work that had been offered only to men in this country (119). The scholastic mode, which emphasizes high standards and rigorous examination, is not egalitarian (115). To open our classes with silence would be a reminder of Bryn Mawr's long-submerged Quaker tradition. I was not at all certain that such a reminder would be appropriate or welcomed by either students or administration here.

Little did I know, as I wrestled with the question of this opening ritual, that silence, in all its complexities, would come to be a vexed theme of my co-teaching with Kaye, that I would quickly lose sight of the ways in which silence could serve as a rich resource for our work together. I became preoccupied instead both with encouraging ourselves and our students to speak up and speak out and with the downside of such practices, the multiple ways in which we were silencing one another. I describe here not only the sometimes-damaging silencing that took place in the course but also my belated rediscovery and recovery of the ways in which silence, as Susan Sontag has said, can not just make words "weigh more," but "keep things open" ("The Aesthetics of Silence" 19–23). I take as my guide in this exploration Gertrude Stein's musing: "silence...respects understanding...silence gives that sense to all there is...Silence is so windowful" (205).

If much of the early work in feminist pedagogy focused on "bringing women to voice" in the classroom, much of the postmodern revisioning has focused on the complexities, difficulties, even the impossibility of doing so. (The foregoing chapter of this volume, which I wrote with Abby Reed, might well be placed in that category. See also the work of Mimi Orner and Elizabeth Ellsworth, who both argue that institutionalized structures prevent genuine sharing of voice in the classroom.) More recently, however, a few pedagogical texts have begun to appear that ask a different question: not just whether it is possible for us to speak of what we know but whether we have overvalued such speaking.

In *Without a Word: Teaching Beyond Women's Silence,* Magda Gere Lewis argues that framing the issue as "getting women to speak" does "not reach deep enough into the sources and political potential of women's silence." She offers instead a conceptual understanding of women's silence "not as a lack" that "reaffirms women's nonexistence, but rather as a source of an active transformative practice" (3, 40, 42). Questioning students' reticence—"probing for details of its generation," recognizing the ways in which it operates as "a form of active resistance" in a "socially untenable position"—Lewis identifies silence as a political practice that challenges how social meaning is made. Reading silence "as a discourse aimed at telling a different story," understanding it as a "counter-language" that carries the full force of opposition to what has been said, Lewis urges women to "publically embrace the politics of absenting" (49, 140).

The essays collected by Elaine Hedges and Shelley Fisher Fishkin in *Listening to the Silences: New Essays in Feminist Criticism* focus not as Lewis does on the oppositional potential of silence but rather on its expressive powers as a corrective to the valorizing of speech and language. Emphasizing the recalcitrance and contingency of the medium of language, the disparity between what is experienced and what it is possible to say, this collection describes silence as a ritual of truth, not to be rewritten and revised but preserved and guarded as a space to think, feel, dream and observe. Silence can lead us to a wider, deeper listening so that the witness of certain books may break our hearts. We may well again grow silent in the presence of such texts (183).

Kaye's and my notions of how silence might operate in the classroom have affinities with the analysis developed by Hedges and Fishkin, but our understanding also has a religious dimension which that collection little explores. We assume a reality of experience, dread-ful, awe-ful, inexpressible, which precedes and evades articulation. In such a world—the world we all occupy—language is not only inadequate as expression; it can also be a hindrance, even a falsification. By beginning each of our classes with several minutes of Quaker silence, we began to hint at such possibilities.

But only to hint at them. Kaye and I quite consciously structured the rest of time we spent with our students less as an interplay of silence and speech than as an exchange between voices. We agreed early on that we had different points of view to offer, many of them a result of our training in different disciplines, and we thought we might best serve the class by playing out these differences frankly and openly. We designed the course as a dialogue between the two of us, attempting to model thereby an interactive conversation which we hoped the students would join.

Our classroom performance was from the first a difficult dance of authority and humility and the choreography was not always smooth. There were a few times when we lost hold of our sense of play, when one of us felt "set up" by the other in class. Students were not always comfortable with our interchange and correction. One said that listening to us was like watching her parents fight, and another complained on her final evaluation: "Sometimes I felt like they tried to one-up the other." Several students used the word "competitive" to describe our interaction, and two said that, while they themselves enjoyed hearing out our differences, their friends did not: "I sort of enjoyed their disagreements, but I can see how others might have found them disruptive." "Anne and Kaye were open about their disagree-ments; that didn't bother me, although I saw others being bothered."

None of these students could quite make sense of a relationship in which there was disagreement without one or the other of us winning the debate. One said, "There was a weird power differential here." As Wayne Koestenbaum observes in *Double Talk*, this language of power, of geopolitics, of territory disputes, the language of war and imperialism, often vexes talk of collaborative work (8). It is even a secondary definition of the word "collaborate": "to cooperate treasonably, as with an enemy occupying one's country" (*The American Heritage*). This meaning connotes compromise, unhealthy allegiances, betrayed trust—all the dangers of interdisciplinary conversation.

For the most part, however, our students found our dialogue instructive. Many of them described our views as "complementary" (this word appeared frequently in their evaluations), and one observed that "they *used* their disagreements to structure class instead of trying to be polite + ignoring them, like some profs do." Talking with each other, Kaye and I found ourselves engaged in a kind of Hegelian discovery of who we were, in opposition to who we were not. For me, this meant a delighted rediscovery of the great value of what I had been working on all along: the imaginative powers of the artist, the expressive powers of language.

We have all heard the most common objection to interdisciplinary work, that it has "no depth." But as Kaye and I articulated the substantial degrees of difference between us, we came to realize that it was precisely those differences that gave our course its depth. At least one student recognized this in her evaluation: "I appreciated that they worked less as 1 coherent prof, than as 2 profs teaching the material—it gave more perspective."

At a Haverford faculty seminar on interdisciplinary teaching, Kaye came to understand how the sort of "binocular vision" encouraged by interdisciplinary work helps all of us see more clearly. Each of our eyes provides a slightly different view of the same scene and together they give us stereoscopic depth perception, enable us better to see three dimensions. Receiving the perspectives of two disciplines, like processing signals from both a right and a left eye, results not in shallow vision but in seeing more deeply.

To create this deeper perspective, and to explain it to our students, Kaye and I had, first, to explain our thinking to one another. We had to learn simpler, clearer ways of saying things, find language that could bridge the gaps between our disciplines, crossover writing and talking that was accessible to non-specialists. Because we kept on talking, we also found that our dialectic was not fixed: we began to move, to appropriate one another's methodologies as a means of understanding an expanded range of objects.

What we were not conscious of at the time, however, but what I became acutely aware of as we continued to work together, were the ongoing silences that marked and exceeded what either of us had to say. Ofttimes our pre-class meetings would be charged with excitement as we tried out our initial, half-formed reactions and ideas on one another. By the time we got to class, we'd smoothed out the rough edges, practiced saying to one another what we intended to repeat to the students and in what sequence. Performing our differences in such a way, I've since learned from Stanley Fish, is to substantially reduce them. Reflecting on Gerald Graff's by-now familiar directive to "teach the conflicts," Fish argues that

> if conflict is made into a structural principle, its very nature is domesticated; rather than being the manifestation of difference, conflict becomes the theater in which difference is displayed and stage-managed. Once a line has been drawn around difference, it ceases to be what it is—the remainder that escapes the drawing of any line, no matter how generous—and becomes just another topic in the syllabus...evading the lesson of its irreducibility. Strange as it may seem, the effect of bringing difference into the spotlight front and center is to obscure its operation. (247–248)

It was not until the end of the class, during each semester we taught the course, that I began to have an awareness of some of the more profound dimensions that had escaped the "domestication" of our "differences" and to perceive them as ominous. Over the course of both semesters, a marked imbalance developed between my speaking and Kaye's silence. Opening class with a period of silence may have well induced me to talk more than I might have otherwise: it gave me time to gather my thoughts, to figure out ways to articulate them forcefully. I also had a second inducement. With a co-teacher always there, sharing my heretofore "privatized" classroom space, I was acutely conscious that my ideas were being heard by a peer and were accountable to her criticism. I spent more time than usual preparing my talks, always aware that Kaye would be there, listening, attentive. I realize now that my keen sense of her as careful listener—for she listens very, very well—made me more voluble in the classroom, eager to get it right, say it right, earn her approval and assent.

When I was a student, I was silent when I had nothing to say. I felt stupid when I was silent. Probably because of such experiences, I tend to read the silence of others in the classroom not just as lack of interest but as lack of ability; conversely, I perform my own engagement in excited speech.

When we repeated our class the following year, I was even more voluble, Kaye even less so. That time 'round, the students' end-of-semester evaluations contained quite a few comments on how I seemed to "dominate," "monopolize," or "take over" our discussions. Two students called that imbalance "unfair," and two others used the language of colonization to express their discomfort: "I felt that Kaye's viewpoint was only privileged as an aside." "It was as though her voice was the 'other.'"

But Kaye's understanding of her silence differed profoundly from that of our students and also from my own. Hers was the insight and the advice of Adrienne Rich's "Cartographies of Silence":

> Silence can be a plan
> rigorously executed...
> It is a presence...
> Do not confuse it
> with any kind of absence.

Kaye's need to keep the conversation going, to fill all the space with talk, was far less pronounced than mine. She was able to step back from constant performance, to give the students time to find their own ways among the tangle of texts and problems we'd posed for them. She was also possessed of a far greater patience than I, a trust that everything did not have to be figured out, much less articulated, within each hour-and-a-half of classroom conversation. I have come only slowly to appreciate what she was much earlier able to understand and to enact. I have done so with her help as well as that of our students, and want to re-trace here several moments in my evolving process of discernment.

At the end of the second week of class, for instance, we assigned three essays, each representing one of the three conventional divisions of academic knowledge. From Sharon Lamb, a psychologist who was one of our predecessors in teaching the course, we had inherited Michelle Fine's essay, "Sexuality, Schooling, and Adolescent Females: The Missing Discourse of Desire." Over and against Fine's exploration of the failure of high school sex education classes in this country to address issues of sexual pleasure, particularly female sexual pleasure, we set two other essays: one written by a Haverford student, Linda Bracci, in which she describes the biological process of orgasm in women, and a short piece by Dorothy Allison called "Femme," which another student had recommended to us as wonderfully, unusually, articulate in describing sexual desire.

At the beginning of class, Kaye invited the students to make our opening silence "impure," to use it for sexual imagining. What sort of language, we then asked, could best express such imaginings? Beginning with Fine's premise—that the articulation of the pleasure of sexual experience is woefully missing from high school sex ed classes—we asked our students to consider the necessity and the value of filling the gap. Why might we need and want to describe sexual pleasure in language? To what degree is the ability to do so an expression of agency? How would they characterize the "discourse of desire" used in each of the assigned essays? What were the capacities and the limitations of each? What other languages might be available to us to describe sexual experience?

We divided the students into small groups and gave them the task of "giving expression to sexual desire" in a way that they could come back and share with the class. Some chose words; one group did a song (giving us all the cites to go with it). Some, who found words inadequate, drew in colored chalk on the board; others tried song, movement, gesture, dance. The students seemed game, the class a lively and joyful one—but afterwards, the newsgroup began to fill with postings describing the difficulty of what we had asked them to do. Looking back through these entries now, I hear them questioning, in a series of linked stages, the fundamental presumption that underlay our structure of that class: the value of bringing sexual desire into speech, of making articulate what we know (or perhaps have not yet known) experientially.

The first student to respond wrote about the marked evasiveness of the words we had used and she had heard in our classroom:

> During Thursday's discussion about desire I noticed that many of us, whether through our writings on the board or out loud, used vague wording to describe our notions of desire. For example, some of the words on the board were "confidence," "heat," "touch," and although each of these words definitely describes feelings of desire, I was wondering why no one was capable of articulating specific actions that describe instances of desire. One group, the one reading pieces of paper from the candy bag, did at times mention such actions, like "being pressed against a wall." But otherwise there was really no mention of actual body parts, particularly those that are usually considered erogenous zones such as the breasts, clitoris, lips, ears. It was funny to think that these body parts, the whole body itself, was left out of a discussion about desire. I don't know about anyone else, but when I think about sexual desire, I don't really think, I feel, and I feel with my body and I feel with certain parts of my body…almost as if they were speaking to me. I also think about certain actions that would make these parts feel good and make me feel good. Why is it so difficult to speak about these actions out loud? Why is it so hard to fill in the blanks: I love when someone _____ my _____ ?

Djung Tran responded to this posting by suggesting that such evasiveness may have been the result of a lack of both experience and understanding. She asked whether she and her classmates knew enough to speak. Their silence, she thought, might mark an unreadiness, an incapacity, an absence:

> when faced with the question of what turns me on, I find I have not asked myself this question with any degree of seriousness, nor do I feel that I have that much direct experience, so I really don't know what to say. I'm not sure if it is more reluctance to reveal myself or not knowing what to reveal. In evaluating the class as a whole I do feel that there…must also be some degree of not knowing what to say or not

unravelling one's feelings so that they can be communicated with sufficient "articulation" to others.

I would like more personal involvedness and frank thoughts in class, but I don't think such an atmosphere springs up immediately, out of nothing...But when someone read the line that went something like "kiss me hard pushed up against the wall," I felt like that came from the gut, and it was immediate and tangible and real, something we could grasp and make something out of. And I think that's what I'm looking for in this class.

Questioning our desire for the sort of language Djung celebrated—that which seemed "immediate and tangible and real"—Penelope Anderson offered the next stage in this examination by challenging our presumption that experience is not valid unless it finds expression in words:

I was thinking about this obligation to articulate that we feel—almost as if language is the only thing that has validity (at least in this academic setting), that movement or other forms of expression cannot exist on their own (no songs without footnotes?). Part of what made me remember this question is my own overwhelming need for language—that it is through and in words that I make sense of the world—in many ways, the way in which I make the world real, make it present to myself. And that dependence (an almost total one) is a limitation of mine. This understanding also, partly, made me realize why articulating desire felt so uncomfortable—putting experiences and feelings into words is always already a means of sharing them, whether anyone else actually reads/listens to them or not, simply because language is a system of shared meanings, of signs mutually understood. And so that trans-lation—that putting desire into language—is also an opening of that desire, a making it manifest and public. And generalizing, in a way—I feel as if I cannot really say, "Well, desire is that smell, of the nape of the neck, and the way your hair curls against my cheek..." because that does not make it, really, and putting desire into language feels too fixed...

Because Penelope was writing her thesis about the possibilities of political poetry, she continued to wrestle with such questions well after our class had ended. If her first e-mail suggested that language might be too "fixed" as an expression of desire, her last one posited the opposite notion: that a particular kind of language, the language of poetry, may be so powerful precisely because it evokes a play of multiple meanings:

> So I am here in the computer center late at night, and realized that I never clarified my point. Poetry cannot imagine that it entirely knows its audience (if it does so posit the audience, I think it fails as poetry): so it must trust to that fragile, transformative nexus of language, that conjunction of poet, poem, and reader, to fundamentally change ways of thinking—not, I think, in ways poet can predict entirely or poem prescribe. Both poetry and polemics want to move, but (I think) successful poetry tends to assume less while trusting to the action of language more. (And it is precisely that trust, that possible multiplicity of meanings, that gives poetry its power.)

Listening to Penelope's reflections again in the silence that opened up when our class and newsgroup discussions ended, it occurs to me that poetry invites the sort of transformation Penelope describes precisely because of the silence that surrounds it, because of all that emptiness on the page. What Penelope terms the "fragile, transformative nexus of language," her call for "trusting to the action of language," depends a great deal on the possibilities offered by the silence that encompasses it, which invites us to "fill in the gaps," to "explicate" what we have heard, by drawing on what we know from our own experience.

Such a process is also a lovely metaphor for what may happen in the classroom, as Judy Logan suggests in her rich collection, *Teaching Stories*: "A good curriculum is like a poem that follows a particular pattern, but that allows the audience to bring their own experiences to the construction of its meaning. It leaves a corner open for the reader to enter" (19). The space on the page around the poem both invites and allows the reader to enter that space where language does not articulate, explicitly, what is meant. The same thing may happen in the space in the classroom—if we can allow it.

The difficulty of doing so was clearly demonstrated, however, the week our class spent discussing Marguerite Duras's novel *The Lover*. Kaye and I had both found the novel elliptical, evasive, irresistibly seductive. Teased and enchanted by its gaps and elisions, we planned our first class with the assumption that our students' experiences of reading would be akin to ours, that they would arrive ready to describe their delighted engagement with the text. We began class by asking them to write for a few minutes about their reading experiences and then asked several of them to read their descriptions aloud. It was soon clear that they had not shared our sense of being "seduced" by the text, and we were flummoxed. We sort of floundered around, not sure where or how to move the conversation forward.

We re-grouped, and Kaye began the following class by describing her own experience of being entranced by the book. I followed up by reviewing two theories of reading. I looked first at the transaction traced by Carla Kaplan in *The Erotics of Talk: Women's Writing and Feminist Paradigms*. Kaplan suggests that all the talk of women coming to voice, of the politics, even the poetics of voice, leaves out a very important dimension of the writing process, that which actually completes it: being heard, by a listener who understands. It is her argument that all narrative is driven by this longing, the force of desire: it is all about "dying to tell/somebody I can talk to." When the transaction works, Kaplan suggests, reading is an erotic experience, what she terms an "erotics of talk. " That was what had happened, I posited, to both Kaye and me as we read *The Lover*.

For the students, however, many of whom felt shut out, disengaged, precisely because the text was so elliptical, the experience of reading was better described by what Judy Butler says in "Gender Is Burning": "'Reading' means taking someone down, exposing what fails to work at the level of appearance, insulting or deriding someone...a reading, an interpretation, appears to be a kind of transparent seeing, where what appears and what it means coincide" (129). Rather than the erotics of reading described by Kaplan, what our students had reported to us was a Butlerian sense of being left out, frustrated, and irritated by the absence of explication in the novel. Kaye and I had found the silences of the text evocative; many of our students had found them, rather, a turn-off. In Kaplan's terms, Kaye and I heard *The Lover* as invitation to listen; in Butler's terms, our students found *The Lover* impossible to read.

One of the students, Megan Munson, offered a way forward from this impasse, by suggesting that any reading could be *made* erotic by the experience of getting intimate with the text, of examining it microscopically...and we were off again: insistently articulating and having our students articulate all the silence evoked. The silences of the text and of the students disappeared, as we labored over what the gaps meant, what they might be made to say to us.

In doing so, we may have lost hold once more of one of the primary values of silence, the capacity of perception it can nurture. This quality is aptly described in Caroline Stephens's analysis of the "result of the practice of silent waiting" in Quaker Meeting for Worship:

> a singularly effectual preparation of mind for the willing reception of any words which might be offered...The words spoken were indeed often feeble, and always inadequate... but, coming as they did after the long silences which had fallen like dew upon the thirsty soil, they went far deeper, and were received into a much less thorny region...one hears harmonies and correspondences...It is sometimes as part-singing compared with unison. (246, 249–250)

Tracing again this sequence of class meetings that made up "Interdisciplinary Perspectives on Gender" — all those silences we fell into and were always trying to work our students out of, all the part-singing we could not hear — I am recalled again to something else I have learned in Quaker Meeting: that the use of language may signal great loss. To reside in silence may be to make oneself available to the mystical. But to speak may violate that experience, as we attempt to express the inexpressible. When silence is embedded in our speaking, we may better hear what is said and better give it voice; moreover, silence alone may be fuller, richer, more replete than language can ever be, an evocation of that which is too full to be spoken, so deep that it defies expression. Marianne Moore observes in her poem "Silence" that people

> can be robbed of speech
> by speech which has delighted them.

The deepest feeling always shows itself in silence;
not in silence, but in restraint.

Quakers celebrate such restraint as a gift, for when we do not speak, we may listen, hear, understand, even communicate in other ways not dependent on speech for fulfillment. If language distorts, silence may open us to revelation. There are mysteries of life known and apprehended only when one refrains from speech, incommunicable mysteries that transcend the capacity of language. As Susan Sontag has said in more secular terms,

> without the polarity of silence, the whole system of language would fail...speech closes off thought. Silence keeps things "open." Still another use for silence: furnishing or aiding speech to attain its maximum integrity of seriousness...when punctuated by long silences, words weigh more. Silence undermines "bad speech"...Words are too crude. And words are also too busy—inviting a hyperactivity of consciousness that is not only dysfunctional...but actively deadens the mind and blunts the senses. Silence...is both the precondition of speech and *the result or aim* of properly directed speech...the artist's activity is...creating silence around things...a full-scale attack on language itself...on behalf of the standard of silence. ("The Aesthetics of Silence" 19–23)

And yet, as our friend and Quaker educator Elaine Crauderueff observes, "We worship in silence. We don't worship the silence." These recurrent themes—openness, silence, space— are all means to an end. Silence is less the "standard" to which we adhere than a way of opening ourselves to revelation. If it is means to an end, the end of knowing the truth, it also marks that end: our ultimate inability to express our understanding of the world, the texts, and the company we keep with one another.

The Quaker understanding of the reflective potential of silence is closely akin to Hannah Arendt's description of the origin of philosophy in speechless "wonder at that which is." Philo-sophers, she posits, differ from others in their capacity "to endure the *pathos* of wonder...Plato proposed to prolong indefinitely the speechless wonder which is at the beginning and end of philosophy. He tried to develop [it] into a way of life" (97,101).

In Arendt's analysis, the philosophic enterprise is initiated but also concludes in speechlessness. At the close of her essay on "Philosophy and Politics," Arendt acknowledges that such speechless wonder has put the philosopher "outside the political realm in which the highest faculty...is...speech" (100). She then begins to speculate about the possibility of developing a "true political philosophy," grounded in the miraculous fact that "'it is not good for man to be alone.'" Arendt postulates that such a practice would make the multiple ways in which we differ from one another, human plurality "in its grandeur and misery," the object of our wonder (103).

This is where Kaye and I are working now, as we figure out how to structure our courses so that they are expressive of Arendt's double insight into our need for both company and silence. Can we make our classes more like our meetings for worship, spaces for a speechlessness that is nonetheless accompanied?

The silences that Kaye remembers most vividly from the course we taught together are not the ones I've recounted above, when we successfully nudged our reluctant students into articulation, but rather those in which some students refused to speak or even chose to excuse themselves from the conversation. Such occasions arose most markedly at the beginning of the course, when we turned our attention to the diseased and dying body.

In response to Caroline Bynum's observation that contemporary academic obsession with "the body" neglected a primary consideration of medieval thinkers, the mortality common to all bodies, we asked our students to read selections from Susan Sontag's *AIDS and Its Metaphors* and Susan Wendell's *The Rejected Body: Feminist Philosophical Reflections on Disability*. We also asked them to watch Bill T. Jones's video *Still/Here*. Sontag questions the value of ascribing metaphors to diseased states because such an attribution may mean finding fault with the victims of disease. Wendell argues that a desire for "transcendence" might express a rational impulse for a sense of self not bound by bodily illness, pain and weakness. Jones conducts workshops for the terminally ill, in which he asks them to enact, by expressing in bodily gestures, their living and their dying. He uses those movements as the basis for his choreography.

Inspired by his work, I wanted to begin our session with a meditation on the moment of our own dying. Kaye suggested wryly that asking our students to imagine the state of their health for the next twenty years might be more than enough of a challenge, as it proved to be. I was surprised to see and hear how strongly the members of our class resisted that exercise and the reflections about normality and vulnerability it provoked. One young woman, who suffers from a chronic but not visible disease, hissed at me, "Why are you making us do this?" Another, whose grandmother was ill, left the class session, because she found the topic so troublingly close to home. It was unclear to us how we could effectively make space in our class for such important topics, without making our students feel that we were forcing them either to speak or to keep away from the discussion.

It wasn't until a year after our co-teaching had ended, when Kaye and I volunteered together for the training offered by the Quaker Ministry for Persons with AIDS, that we began to understand how the structure of our classes—not any particular way they were structured but the very existence of a reliable structure, of a commitment to come together regularly to discuss texts and topics of common interest and as regularly disperse—might address both the common condition of our loneliness and the imperative to reflect on our multiple differences.

In the last chapter, I explicitly resisted Abby's request for a "prescription," arguing that no structure can accommodate the needs of all those who gather within it, that each re-formation will produce its own resistance. But I want to set alongside that insight its opposite: that a faithful commitment to structure itself, an assurance that we will meet regularly and labor together—as well as a willingness to let go, not to push the conversation too far, to be too intrusive—may provide the only opening we need.

One afternoon during our AIDS training, I was assigned the role of counselor to another volunteer: Kathy Corbett was enacting the position of a depressed patient, full of pity for herself. Overwhelmed by her portrayal of the depressed patient's helplessness, I could think of nothing to say, could only repeat that I would be returning to visit for four hours each week, that we would then see what happened.

Kathy reported afterwards not only that her longing for connection increased as I waited in silence with her but also that she found succor in simply being reminded of the structure available to her without any promise or prediction of what might happen during our time together. In the newsletter of the Quaker Ministry, Mary Lou Phillips testified similarly to her eight months of visits with her client: "I was faithful, which is most of what he wanted from me" (7).

It seems to us now that our classrooms, too, function most simply, and most wondrously, as spaces where such faithful attentiveness is enacted, as antechambers that may serve as entryways into—who knows what?—to understandings that will eventually emerge. Kaye and I celebrate the labor but also the wonder of this potential encounter as we come together regularly in classes with our students, for visits with our AIDS patients and in meetings for worship with our religious community.

Our Quaker meeting is a gathering of friends who share no common understanding of God—there are atheists, agnostics, universalists, Christians, Jews, and Buddhists of many stripes among us—but we come together in the commonality of search. As one of our members, Walter Smedley, said, "You can hear the anvils beating" each Sunday morning as we struggle to make sense of our lives. When they are working, something similar may go on in our classes.

We revel in the classroom because it is a place of escape from the messiness and diffuseness of everyday life—but also a place where such messes get attended to and clarified. A group of people agree to come together, on a regular, predictable but limited schedule—and these limits are important. They allow for, encourage, the focus of our conversations. We love the concentrated intensity.

Why do we do this work? It is a call into conversation and a stepping out of dialogue. A clarity. A confusing. A loving. An obsession. Both succor and escape.

Gargoyle. Cloisters. Thomas Hall. Bryn Mawr College.
Photograph by Carlos Garcia. 2001.

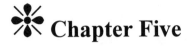 # Chapter Five

"Turtles All the Way Down": Class as Persistent Critique

In 1985, Bryn Mawr instituted a program for older women returning to college; they are called "McBride Scholars" in honor of Katherine McBride, a past president of the college. For many years, my colleague Susan Dean taught a first-year writing course for the McBrides. When I inherited the course from her, I inherited with it an important essay by the anthropologist Clifford Geertz called "Thick Description: Toward an Interpretive Theory of Culture." In it, Geertz reports

> an Indian story...about an Englishman who, having been told that the world rested on a platform which rested on the back of an elephant which rested in turn on the back of a turtle, asked...what did the turtle rest on? Another turtle. And that turtle? "Ah, Sahib, after that it is turtles all the way down." (28–29)

Geertz uses the story to illustrate his point that all cultural inquiry is unfinished, that the further he gets into any project, the more unfinished it is, the more he learns he has left to know:

> Nor have I ever gotten anywhere near to the bottom of anything I have ever written about ...Cultural analysis is intrinsically incomplete. And, worse than that, the more deeply it goes the less complete it is...to commit oneself to...an interpretive approach...is to commit oneself to a view of ethnographic assertion as..."essentially contestable." Progress is marked less by a perfection of consensus than by a refinement of debate. What gets better is the precision with which we vex each other. (29)

My first group of McBrides soon figured out that I was putting them up to the same business. Inevitably, when one of them submitted a paper to me, I'd say, "Good, as far as you go—now try going further, in this (or that) direction." Inevitably, when another made a point in class, I'd say, "Good—and that raises yet another question." And so Geertz's story became a joke, a tag, a leitmotif for our work together.

During our last session, the students presented me a T-shirt with a tortoise on it. Since that time, subsequent classes of McBrides have adopted a turtle at the Philadelphia Zoo and given me a range of related gifts: turtle pins and stickers, plastic and ceramic turtles (including a stack built by a student-artist), a turtle Christmas ornament, a nervous turtle shaking in its box, a postmodern turtle puzzle, a pad of turtle paper, a turtle magnifying glass, turtle earrings, bracelets and pins and a turtle made of tomato aspic. (We ate that gift as we celebrated the semester's end.) My family has added to the collection with more jewelry and a turtle blanket.

The remnants of my turtle collection sit now interspersed among the books in my office, and I often invoke them metaphorically in conversation and in class as I invite new McBrides into an ever-expanding and never-ending process of inquiry. In turn, they invite me to consider further resonances which the image evokes for them. One McBride, for instance, used the turtle, first in poetry, then in prose, to explore her notion of a layered self, "boundless, cosmic," in the process of uncovering.

Sarah Campbell.
Emergen/t/c/y

> Pregnant title waves
> Topple these temples,
> Pounding them to sandcastles
> From which one lone turtle tracks toward the sea.
>
> A gentle breath.
> Another surge—urgent,
> And firm hands
> Cradle sure this temp'st borne surfling
> Emerging from the sea in me:
> my self.

The Voice of the Turtle

I have always been drawn to turtles. I like their pace—somewhere between bumble and mosey, and their intent—between indolence and resolve. And that instant voyage they make from outer world to inner. Clap! And they are safe, sealed up in that cozy inner room while who knows what or who buffets beyond the door. The turtle and I, or the turtle in me, always kept a secret: that her sealed-up inner room is actually larger than the world outside, larger by far. Boundless, cosmic, with paths that meander through thoughts arranged like the inside of pomegranate, one juicy cell opening up into myriad others. The true reality; it is the outside world that is virtual...

I found this borne out in Greek mythology, where I recently located the turtle back at the very beginning of things. The god Hermes, the messenger of the gods, meets a turtle. Hermes does something very interesting. He makes it into a lyre.

Around the table on the porch of English House we have delved into the deeps of written word to find just how far down we could dive, with turtles marking the fathoms of our descent. But have they been just outer turtles, appearing only in what we read? Haven't we all encountered some inner ones, who appear in what we write?

I have wondered that about myself, as some music comes forth in a paper, some turn of mind, some tune I didn't know I was humming. Now I know, I say, Ah! Hermes, that messenger angel. The voice of the turtle. But which turtle is this? And how far down do they go?

Anne

Prodded by Sarah's musings, I want to pause, three-fourths of the way through this book, and dive a bit into the "boundless" self who offers the sort of classes I have been describing here in such detail. What follows, in the form of a collage, are the defining stories of my teaching life. They describe my own affective investments and so tell what fuels this enterprise for me: what I am seeking in the classroom, what brings me into that space, again and again, with such hope (and drives me out of it in despair).

"Sometimes the smallness of what I do shames me." (Mary Gordon, *Spending: A Utopian Divertimento* 81)

Sometimes the enormity of what I am trying to do overwhelms me.

I would go in to my grandmother early in the morning when she'd slept over. Slipping up to the side of her bed, book in hand, I asked her to read to me. She always said "yes." (Did she never say "no"? Did she sometimes want to?)

I was a child who loved to read. Where there was no reading culture.

I was raised in a small town in northwestern Virginia; my family and their friends were housewives, farmers, small businessmen. Not drawn to the kinds of work they did—in part as an escape from that sort of labor—I read voraciously. Books gave me some understanding of the world I lived in; they also served as entry into other, larger worlds than the one we inhabited.

My family were conscientious people, but the limits of their concern and compassion were clearly marked. They attended faithfully, extensively, to those they knew, those like themselves. Our warm and caring community had an outside, sharply drawn.

In this first story about my teaching, I learn the limits of my teachers.

I am a cheerleader. The squad hosts a party for the football team in my home. The next season, we want to have one for the basketball players, some of whom are black—did I mention that we are white? My father refuses. So do the fathers of the other white girls. Socializing leads to dating; dating leads to marriage. The folly of mixing the races. Quotes about breeding (racehorses, I think).

How do I know this is wrong? Where does that knowledge come from?

We host the party in the school cafeteria. The girls' team asks why we haven't had one for them as well. I see the racism clearly then. Not yet the sexism.

What enables my understanding? What marks its boundaries?

I leave home in the summer of 1968 as an exchange student to the small city of Schleswig in northern Germany. The family who takes me in asks lots of questions—about Methodists, Republicans, Americans, what "we" think of the work of Martin Luther King. Their queries lead me to re-examine much I have never questioned before. This may have been when doubt—corrosive, liberating—takes hold. And never ends.

College next. Freshman writing. We're reading a Hemingway short story; the prof is criticizing the staccato dialogue between husband and wife. When I defend it as appropriate to this exchange, Professor Fehrenbach responds, "ALL of Hemingway's characters talk that way." And the world suddenly opens up for me into a maze of texts. I realize that, to speak with authority about this one story, I need to read them all.

And so I become an English major and begin to read sort of conversationally, sort of systematically, as each text leads me into the others which inform it.

There is another impulse. I am in love with a poet. I become an English major so I can talk with him. I have no idea what I think, what to look for, how to "read" the poems he gives me, how to answer the questions he asks. This is English major as entry into relationship.

But after a year or two, I become impatient with the structure, the tedium of studying what others think I should know.

> *"Most people, most of the time, experience schooling as 'dreary*
> *tiresome days.'"* (Philip Corrigan, *Social Forms/Human*
> *Capacities* 157).

I quit, marry the poet, get a job. Try reading on my own for a few
years. But I keep falling asleep, and begin to realize how much I
need the dialogue of the classroom, the context of a conversation.
Looking for someone to talk to, I go back to college.

But I develop a growing impatience with grandstanding, with
anyone who talks too much, for too long, who doesn't invite a
dialogue.

Does telling my own stories this way invite dialogue? Or close it
off?

> *Linda Kauffman insists that the testimony of personal experience*
> *is a way of muzzling dissent: "difficult to resist is the temptation*
> *to view the personal as inherently paradigmatic...It makes us see*
> *similarity where in fact there are only...irresolvable, irreconcil-*
> *able differences."* ("The Long Goodbye: Against Personal
> Testimony, or An Infant Grifter Grows Up" 1156, 1159)

This is experience as conversation stopper: when we treat what
we know experientially as privileged, believing that knowledge
rooted in experience is unassailable. What authority am I claiming
by telling these tales? What conversations am I shutting down?

My husband and I move to Philadelphia; he begins law school at
Penn. I work as a secretary in the financial aid office. Am bored.
Take a graduate course (free to employees): Faulkner and James.
Wonderful weeknights, reading on the sofa. Wonderful weekend
afternoons, writing papers.

I apply to the graduate program in English; get in; go. At one of
those early, scary parties, I tell the chairman about my class with
Barbara Herrnstein Smith. He mishears me—thinks I've punned

her middle name as "Hermeneutics"—and laughs heartily. I have no idea what hermeneutics ARE, and am embarrassed, at having gotten credit for a joke I 1) have not made and 2) worse—do not understand.

Credit for jokes—this may be emblematic of the anxieties of graduate work.

There are many pleasures too: reading to hear stories I haven't heard. Teaching and inviting others to do the same: listening to the tales of those who have been silent.

But, slowly, the work comes to seem arid, unrelated to the questions I am asking about the patterns of my life. My mother-in-law is having a nervous breakdown, my cousins begin having children. I want to attend to the old; I want to care for the young.

What do my studies have to do with these wants, these needs?

The classes don't interest me. They don't seem to interest the professors, either. A professor begins a Melville seminar by asking, "Is this the book with Long John in it?" We grad students work up a riff: "Is This the Book about the Whale?"

What do these men have to teach me?

At the end of the first year, I drop out of school, start working as a secretary in the English Department. I am aghast to see how much focus there is on hierarchies, gate-keeping, one-upmanship.

> *"I'd met philosophers, thinkers, theater people...I knew artists and poets...famous explorers...eminent scientists...people who in many respects were fascinating. But...genius...was not necessarily accompanied by what you could call human perfection. All their talent, all their intellectual and artistic skills, didn't necessarily make them good human beings...the mastery such people possessed in their particular field was often not matched by even the simplest human perfections—like altruism, goodness,*

or sincerity." (Matthieu Ricard in Revel and Ricard, *The Monk and the Philosopher* 6)

It seems paradoxical to me that English professors could be inhumane. I do not yet understand how the pursuit of excellence and mastery in a discipline fosters such behavior.

> *Peggy McIntosh explains how this training works:* "The winners are few, and high up on narrow bit of land which are the peaks; the losers are many and are low down...Both our public institutions and collective as well as innermost psyches have taken on the hierarchical structure of this winning-versus-losing kind of paradigm...the actual liberal arts function... is...to train a few students to climb up to pinnacles. The territory of excellence is very small." ("Interactive Phases of Curricular Re-Vision" 127–128)

> *Like McIntosh, Parker Palmer has a counter-proposal, argues for the* "urgent need in this world for styles of education which will raise up peacemakers, inventors of new futures, and persons confident of their own humanity—not competitors, consumers, and diminished selves." ("Meeting for Learning" 6)

I take a year off but then return to graduate school. What draws me back? Something that lasts: a desire to keep on learning.

> *In doing so, I follow Gayatri Spivak, prodded to* "think about the danger of what is useful...the critique of things...without which we cannot live...the persistent critique of what one must inhabit." (Outside in the Teaching Machine 4, 10, 61)

Larry Ziff passes through the English Department at Penn, opens up my reading of literature into a reading of history, makes the field seem much larger. He names my work women's studies. I'm surprised by the category, haven't conceptualized it that way. Didn't know that such a field exists.

I am awarded a Mellon Fellowship, go to the reception, start up a conversation. Get in over my depth. Feel my own silence. As dumbness.

I'm writing my dissertation. Soon find myself bored, again, with this tiny little project. How have I dug myself into such a deep, narrow hole? The questions I am asking-and-trying to answer seem very small ones, of interest to very few people. What has happened to the exhilarating sense of expanse with which I'd first embraced this process?

> *"To borrow a phrase from St. Augustine: 'I want to stir our souls, not test our ingenuity as lockpicks.'"* (Daryl Koehn, *Rethinking Feminist Ethics* 157)

> *"I came to see research, as I experienced it myself, as an endless dispersion into detail, and dedicating my whole life to it was something I could not longer envisage...For me, the mass of scientific knowledge had become 'a major contribution to minor needs.'"* (Ricard in Revel and Ricard 2, 12)

I work on, staying at home, not getting out much. Sometime after the birth of my first child, I return to a grad student gathering. I feel the lively engagement of the others, feel again the heaviness of my own silence, my out-of-the-loopness. I don't know—already, just one year later—don't know what they know. Can't enter the conversation.

> *Renato Rosaldo re-tells Kenneth Burke's "parable of a conversation that goes on before, during, and after any talker's lifetime: 'Imagine that you enter a parlor. You come late. When you arrive, others have long preceded you, and they are engaged in...a discussion too heated for them to pause and tell you exactly what it is about...You listen for a while, until you decide that you have caught the tenor of the argument; then you put in your oar. Someone answers; you answer him; another comes to your defence; another aligns himself against you... the discussion is*

interminable. The hour grows late, you must depart. And you do depart, with the conversation still in progress.'" (104)

Putting in one's oar is often difficult. Throughout these defining tales, I hear, recurring, the motif of exclusion. I want to be included, myself. And I want to hear the voices that have not been listened to.

The graveyard at The Old Chapel in Boyce, Virginia, is full. Susan Dean's brother is being buried just outside the gates. Wandering around, before his memorial service, I find a marker in (the back right-hand corner of) the cemetery:

> To the Glory of God
> And in Remembrance of the Many Personal
> Servants Buried Here Before 1865.
>
> Faithful and Dedicated in Life, Their Friends
> And Masters Laid Them Near Them in Death,
> With Affection and Gratitude.
>
> Their Memory Remains, Though Their Wooden Markers,
> Like the Way of Life of That Day,
> Are Gone Forever.
>
> I.T.G. 1957

The silence is deafening.

My evolution into teaching-as-I-do-it now goes through several stages after I arrive at Bryn Mawr, fueled by a growing awareness that the traditional questions structuring the field of English— what is great literature, who defines the terms, whose needs they serve, the whole notion of literature as the best that has been thought and said (so leaving out the experiences of most of the world's peoples)—have become problematic for me. The categories defining the English major seem increasing false: I realize what a small island England is, from a global perspective, how nationalistic it is to organize a discipline in those terms. I begin to design courses that use literature to ask different—what seem to me larger, more important—questions.

Do not seek to hold me, for it is too strait for me; and out of this straitness I must go, for I am wound into largeness. (Ernest Taylor 3)

I overhear a colleague, whose office is next door. He asks his travel agent to book his flight using the title "Dr." "Then they won't bump me. They won't bump a doctor." I find jarring his sense of the importance of "doctors of philosophy." Why should we *not* be bumped?

Jarring, too, is his reaction to my third pregnancy. He thinks that the elite should be reproducing at a higher rate. I can't believe what I'm hearing: *mine* are the genes we need more of?

I dislike overhearing myself, telling these stories on a co-worker. But such perceptions fuel my teaching, direct its focus on patterns of exclusion.

Is that also a pattern I reproduce by telling these stories? Trying to control the conversation? To correct my colleagues?

Gina Dent considers confession a means of policing borders: "disguised underneath it are often attacks against those who stand outside of the circle...[attempts] to gain the authority to take control of our collective stories." ("Missionary Position" 71, 74)

I think of the tales my Virginia family is always telling on one another, stories insistently fueled by our love for each other. Yet, too: the storytelling marks the limits of our love and acceptance.

Each of the chapters of this book, so far, ends with the same gesture. An echo resonates from Isaac Penington, who speaks of our life as "love, and peace, and tenderness," to Luce Irigaray, describing "a style of loving relationships"; from Audre Lorde, on the hunger of loving "easily," to Kaye Edwards and I on the work we do: "A loving. An obsession." What's love got to do with it?

In Gypsy Academics and Mother-Teachers: Gender, Contingent Labor, and Writing Instruction, *Eileen Schell argues that an economic reality lies behind this "mystified argument for the 'pedagogy of maternal love'": our willingness to work for lower wages than men (33, 24). She quotes Redding Sugg's* Motherteacher: *"The first profession opened to women consisted of the sale of sexual love and was called prostitution; the second...was a traffic in maternal love and was called pedagogy." (20)*

Schell debunks the "destructive myth" of part-time work for "psychic income," a sense of satisfaction and fulfillment that can function as part of one's compensation. She challenges the stereotype of the dabbling housewife, whose intellectual work is unconnected to her status as worker. Not personal choices, Schell argues, but structural factors — "sex-role socialization, market demands, hiring practices, and sex-discrimination" — hold such women back from full-time careers. At considerable price: a "loss of control of one's working conditions, hence one's academic freedom." (36, 40–41, 49, 119)

This is me. I am the bored housewife. Working for pin money. Not in control of the structures of my employment. The operative paradigm here, the template of value, is that of full-time work, which I have refused.

I am in the midst of lamenting, late one afternoon, about being left out of campus decision-making. Linda-Susan Beard shakes her head: "I can't imagine what it must be like to go through the world as a white woman."

I try to imagine, try to say: what IS it like, to be a woman who is white? And well-(enough)-to-do, with a husband, a-poet-when-I-married-him, now turned corporate lawyer? The freedom, what Simone de Beauvoir calls the "incomparable privilege" of "irresponsibility": not "having" to work, working not for money, but for the satisfaction of doing something that seems important, something that engages.

De Beauvoir denounces such a position: "Free from troublesome burdens and cares...without ever being impressed with the necessity of taking charge of [our] own existence. [This is] complicity...cowardice...[we must] transcend our assigned role." (The Second Sex 801–802)

Eventually it comes clear to me that the way I live my life outside class—the way I attend to my family, the sort of social justice work I do, the way I worship—very much informs what I teach, the way I teach. I make a conscious decision to bring that life, those values, into the class—not to be a disembodied reader of texts, teaching others how to read carefully, performing purely intellectual exercises, but asking my students to reflect on what our reading has to do with the sorts of people they are becoming.

"Conventional education...supposedly deals with only a narrow slice of our selves, a trainable bunch of abilities and skills... Of course, that is an illusion. In most schools people pay a high emotional price in terms of self-image and self-confidence...Whatever the subject of study in a classroom the shadow subject is ourselves, our limits, our potentials." (Parker Palmer, "Meeting for Learning" 5)

Bryn Mawr faculty begin a series of conversations about "the global curriculum." At one of the sessions, a member of the (insistently European) Art History Department declares that she is not nor does she want to be "an undergraduate generalist." In her renunciation, I hear described the sort of academic I will become. It's not the operative template on campus, but one I take up with great pleasure.

I enjoy immensely the range of work available to an "undergraduate generalist": helping first-year students learn how to write, introducing older women to college study, offering a range of courses that question gender roles as well as those that explore the perpetually expanding canon of American literature. I become as interested in my students as in the texts I offer them for study and interested in the texts as a way of helping students think about who they are, who they want to be, what role they will play in the world.

> *"Part-time faculty may put far more time and energy into a single course and into working with individual students than a full-time faculty member would...As a group they profess to be far less discipline- or knowledge-centered than full-time faculty and far more interested in helping students learn, grow, and develop."* (Gappa and Leslie, *The Invisible Faculty* 224)

But I often feel myself caught between the demands of teaching and those of mothering. Trying to be fully present to a student with whom I am meeting (for example), I can never hold a conference without a consciousness of what is going on elsewhere, in the spheres where I am responsible. Which child needs to be fetched and carried, when? where? How to attend to all the matters simultaneously needing attention?

I take this concern—at that point, a full-fledged anxiety, for I am all the time anxious—to the Co/n-spiritors, a group of faculty who gather monthly to discuss the intersections of our academic and spiritual lives. Susan Dean reminds me of the archetypal fairy tale: the story of the third son who gets the reward because he is willing to linger along the way, attending to whatever, whomever asks for help en route. Paying attention to what is before us is the best way to arrive where we want to go in the end. That tale strikes me with the force of revelation: the need to be present to the task at hand. My failure—and my longing—to do so.

I like the way the classroom answers that need, by calling us momentarily out of life's distractions and interruptions. I like the coming together—I'm surprised, each time I show up, that the students have, too—to talk about important things, texts that invite us to reflect on the meanings of our lives. In our classroom, we gather together over books we love.

Sometimes they hate the books I pick. Don't read them. Don't care.

"One purpose of a liberal arts education is to make your head a more interesting place to live inside of for the rest of your life." (Mary Patterson McPherson, past president of Bryn Mawr College)

Talking with Brenda, who teaches high school English, over our driveway fence. Her students are "pretending to take" honors courses. "Pretending to read."

Susan Dean speaks in a faculty group about the "violence of being too knowing." Reflecting on how hard it is for first-year students, with every constituent of self in question, to write a knowing essay, she proposes that we "adjust our paper requirements to allow for not knowing," "for personal questions, misgivings raised by a text." She describes her own attempts to counter the professionalism we were taught, and teach: papers that are narrow in focus, contained, knowing, produced by a self that is discrete.

> *"...not a coherent viewpoint but a mind deeply and mysteriously in conflict with itself."* (Ruth Yeazell's description of Charlotte, in *Language and Knowledge in the Late Novels of Henry James* 9)

One of my graduate profs asks me if I'm from the South. He hears "the accent, but only sometimes"; I drop it when I'm speaking more formally, more academically.

My cousin Carolyn says, "This doesn't sound like Anne." Kaye Edwards says, "You seem to have multiple audiences." Another colleague, Alison Cook-Sather, suggests that "multiple audiences are good."

> *Kamala Visweswaran describes the time it has taken her "to realize that different audiences might require different forms of writing and theorizing."* (11)

I first conceive this project as a conversation between myself and others with whom I work, both students and teachers. I want to write with the corrective of others' points of view, not trusting myself to give an accurate or complete-enough picture of what is happening in my classrooms.

> *I want to avoid the danger Ann Hulbert describes in her review of Vivian Paley's book,* The Kindness of Children: *"Paley has been a teacher with a faith, not a lesson plan: a faith that through the shaping and sharing of stories comes comprehension... stories can work to draw a class together and lead children out of loneliness...They have told their teacher...much...over the years, and she always listened—until her turn came to do most of the talking."*

> *"In most educators' writing, I can't see a student for miles around. It takes my breath away to open a book on education and find it so peopled."* (Peggy McIntosh, Afterword to Judy Logan's *Teaching Stories* 159)

But what I discover as I write and then wait, first patiently, then impatiently, for the responses of my colleagues, is that I too-insistently call for them (telling them when they should speak, even, often, what I think they had to say), not really giving them space to do so.

With some shock, I come across an old e-mail from another colleague: "You are making me feel bullied and labeled and just plain bad. I am now, for the last time...asking you to respect those feelings as you respond to my request for silence. Couldn't you, as my friend, please do that?"

How often have my friends resented my questions, resisted the direction I give our conversation?

I lose my footing with this project. My collaborators have gone silent. Linda-Susan Beard suggests I re-conceive the dialogue as internal, report my sharp sense of dividedness: between what I do and what-I-think-others-are doing, what I do and what-I-think-I should-do, what I do and what I think, what I think and what I think.

> *"If resistance is always the sign of a counter-story, ambivalence is perhaps the state of holding on to more than one story at a time."* (Barbara Johnson, *The Feminist Difference* 2)

I hear this story from another colleague, Helene Elting. Her mother is dying of breast cancer. She is going to New York each weekend to care for her, then returning to Bryn Mawr, exhausted, to teach. One of those weary mornings, she sees our department chairman, muses, "Maybe I should tell my class what is going on. Apologize for my absence of attention, my not-really-being-here." He replies: "I never start a conversation in my classes, if I don't know where it's going to go."

His comment is a reminder of the advice Helene and I got from our graduate teaching instructor at Penn: "Never ask a question in class if you don't know the answer."

Nowadays I *only* ask a question in class if I do not know the answer. Otherwise, what's the point? I want to be in conversations going somewhere I haven't been before, teaching me something I don't yet know. If I come into class knowing what will happen, knowing everything they should know, and serve it up, where's the space for discovery?

Writing this book, though, trying to script what happens on these pages—*how, otherwise, will I ever get anything written?*—I realize how insistently I still script my classroom conversations. I ask leading questions and insist that my students answer them.

> *"Of course, we depend on teachers to help us explore possibilities and express complexity. That's what they were after with their questions...Your simple sentences did not raise the questions; your teachers did."* (Michael Downing, *Perfect Agreement* 119)

In The Other Side of Language: A Philosophy of Listening, *Gemma Fiumara observes that "the question...predetermines or circumscribes the answer it receives...the way in which a question is posed limits and conditions the quality, and level, of any answer that can be possibly worked out...it is not clear whether...the question is authentically open...the grave contractual weight of the question is beginning to be felt." (34, 37)*

I begin to recognize the stark limits of my class discussions. I invite students to speak, then am disappointed when they don't say what I want them to. Me as ventriloquist.

Throughout these defining tales, I hear, recurring, the motif of inclusion. My classes are driven by my need to hear the voices that have not been listened to. If silent students do not speak, I cannot know whether they are satisfied. I attempt to ferret that out—realizing, oh-so-belatedly, the violence of that insistence, that persistence, that curiosity of mine. *Why* it is so important for me for them (all) to talk? Am I just looking for authorization/affirmation/confirmation of my own speaking?

E-mail from Andrea Miller, 10/5/98: When we were in early discussions about this project, I had this fuzzy ambivalent feeling about publishing...But when I read your draft, the focus suddenly sharpened. I felt like the safely hypothetical/tentative/experimental student was about to be dragged out of the conference room and into a spotlight...I wondered if you had recruited me to lend legitimacy to laying all this out...a showy enterprise...for the world to see.

Five months later, Andrea stepped out of the project: "I cannot write in this framework. I do not want to play the role you have assigned me in this narrative of your education as a teacher."

Freire says, "The teacher's thinking is authenticated only by the authenticity of the students' thinking...Authentic thinking...[takes] place...only in communication." (Pedagogy of the Oppressed 64)

Andrea writes, "I think the nature of the project of writing about the classroom distorts perspective. This is what I mean: there is so much good about what you do in the classroom, so much that works — but these are not 'issues' so they go largely unexamined. The 'issues' are hot, conflicted, uncomfortable, unresolved, and so they go through endless scrutiny. The final impression is that everything is wrong with the classroom, which is certainly not near to the truth."

I don't much trust myself. Don't trust what I know.

> *Spivak might call that "responsibility": "proceeding from an awareness of the limits of one's power...what I cannot imagine stands guard over everything that I must/can do, think, live."* (Outside in the Teaching Machine *10, 22)*

> *Kauffman says, "the older I get, the less I'm able to construct a moral even to my own story that doesn't lie with every word... we still have the most to learn from the ruptures, limitations, and contradictions in our thinking." She suggests enacting "a conscious strategy of...'infidelity': one can show how one's own argument may subsequently become inadequate."*

> *I follow her here, and Sandra Harding, who likewise exhorts us "to engage in traitorous readings of the assumptions we make...continually to cast doubt on the status of knowledge— even as we are in the process of constructing it—a perpetual project."* (Linda Kauffman *1159, 1167–1168)*

I follow, too, the McBrides, who testify, over and over again, to the unremittingness of this search. And to its costs.

Belkys López. Turtle Storm
　　Picture turtles being flung at you from every direction, some knocking you on your head. Kamikaze turtles diving at you. And there you are trying to catch them. But you can't. They're too heavy and there are too many turtles for your eyes to target one.

But at least you are getting the opportunity to glance at them. If someone were to ask you what a turtle is, having been knocked on the head by one, you would be able to answer, "Oh, yes, a turtle is an animal with a hard shell, somewhat greenish in color and not at all graceful in the air." Turtles are creatures that normally travel slowly on the ground and usually not in herds or packs. But at Bryn Mawr we come in contact with turtles that travel in large numbers and at high velocity. Bryn Mawr is in the turtle-flinging business.

I've been bruised by turtles. Now I wonder why my contact with turtles has to take this frenzied form. The standard has been set before us. The women who graduate from Bryn Mawr can catch flying turtles with the best. Bryn Mawr is acclimating women to the type of schedule they will be expected to run on in the work world. All this high-volume turtle catching is in line with the mass production ideology of corporate America. Bryn Mawr students going out into the work force will be well conditioned to make the sacrifices that employees are expected to make for their jobs.

We need to question the value system operating at Bryn Mawr. What is the value of giving more reading than a student can possibly do? Or asking students to churn out papers in an assembly-line fashion? Education shouldn't be like mass production.

I will continue at Bryn Mawr, trying to maneuver my way through this turtle storm, glancing at some and spending more time with others. Although my experience here has been a bit frenzied, still I have had some exquisite moments of revelation. I will continue, though I am disturbed by the bombardment. I'm being challenged by the turtles. I don't want to turn away from the challenge.

Jennifer Bopp. The End of Mawrtyrdom

"The means and ends of education"—this is exactly what has been troubling me during my first year at Bryn Mawr College. My earlier years of study were generally happy ones. When I entered the university, I felt as though I had discovered a buried and essential part of myself. I was a passionate, almost euphoric, student who worked hard. When I was out of school for breaks, I felt anxious and dissatisfied. Christmas break seemed too long. I always took (and enjoyed) summer courses. I liked the prospect of learning new things. Each semester offered a whole new opportunity. I felt like a kid in a candy store every time I selected my next semester's classes. When I reached the end of my sophomore status, I felt startled; I had merely been doing something which I enjoyed. Certainly, I felt elation and pride for having reached the halfway point. But there was an odd melancholia mixed in with my jubilant emotions. By acknowledging this halfway point, I realized, with some dismay, that there would be an end.

Something changed when I transferred to Bryn Mawr College. I was no longer the kid in the candy store. Bryn Mawr representatives told me insistently that I would need to achieve a certain level of mathematics, "x" number of courses in athletics, and several years of a language or I wouldn't graduate from Bryn Mawr. There it was—that focus on "the end." I felt no more ambivalence about that end to education—I wanted it. And it seemed impossibly far away.

I was always a very hard worker. I generally worked beyond what professors requested of me. I had a good deal of room to make education my own; what I put into my education, I got back. I expected Bryn Mawr to be more demanding. I wanted to be challenged. I wanted to grow. But I soon found Bryn Mawr College to be so demanding I could hardly think or act outside of studying. I studied ALL THE TIME. Whereas my life had previously seemed expanded by education, it now was somehow diminished. My professors demanded so much work from me and fed me so much information, that my tendency to "do more" (to make education my own) left me lifeless.

From time to time I let loose a flood of desperation and despair. My friends and family would respond, "Well, just try to hang in there. Come on, just grit your teeth and get through it. Just a couple of years and it will be over." So it seems that education is something through which I must suffer. I must sacrifice heavily to make it to the end. I finally understood that moniker of the Bryn Mawr student: *mawrtyr.*

I think the problem is that I don't believe that education should end. It seems that colleges and universities believe that students will only be learning for those several years of enrollment. Since the period of learning is limited, the college must deluge the student with as much reading, writing, and hard work as a human body and mind can stand. As if there is no tomorrow. Then the student gets a degree. Then the student can stop learning. After the battle of such educational experience, it would be no surprise if the student never again wanted to pick up a book.

I don't want to pray for a merciful end of education. I don't want to believe that education is about death rather than life. Can I be a Bryn Mawr student without being a *mawrtyr?*

Claudia Leiva. Straight Line-Anne, Zig-Zag Claudia

I am exhausted by the amount of writing I have to do in English 016. I have pushed myself to the edge so I can accomplish my task of writing a well-done, a structural, and a clear English paper for the future and the present. But I am really tired. I was never confronted with such a predicament in my life. I could not understand why Anne was being so strict to me. I felt completely vulnerable. It was like when you have that dream that you are naked in the middle of a dance room and every single person in the room is staring at you. I felt like that about English class.

Fortunately, it was just a dream. On Sunday afternoon, as I was reading a book entitled *This Bridge Called My Back: Writing by Radical Women of Color* by Cherrie Moraga and Gloria Anzaldua. I saw at the bottom of the page a footnote that saved my life. It says,

> English expository writing goes in a straight line...from introductory paragraph, to thesis sentence, to conclusion. Spanish composition follows a form more like a zig-zag, sometimes deviating from straight, linear thinking. I am fighting against this when I write in English so I can be understood by English readers. (Moschkovich 82)

I am not alone anymore. I felt like a zig-zag trying to follow a straight line.

Myra Reichel. works in progress
this is a sad and perplexing problem—my writing seems to get less and less under my

control and has become a chore of placing thoughts in sequence. I have a great desire for

it to be what it is not. I am not sure whether this writing on the computer is as helpful as it

seems since I am dependent on it to the extent that my thinking seems to only progress

while I am typing and at a standstill at other times. I guess I need more contact with the

other students in order to think on my feet. The thoughts seem OK in my head but go

through an impossible birthing process where I am confused whether I am throwing away

the baby or the afterbirth.

Connectedness. Sculpture, Bryn Mawr College.
Milan Kralik. 1990.
Photograph by Carlos Garcia. 2001.

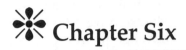 **Chapter Six**

"The Form of a Longing":
Class as Falling in and out of Love

This...could be called the...falling-in-love model...of
teaching and learning...It is Platonic or Freudian. Or
perhaps infectious...Teacher as...someone you want to eat
or someone you want to eat you—to love or be loved.
> Peter Elbow, "The Pedagogy of the
> Bamboozled" 96

Sometimes the feelings I have toward my students are
romantic. It's like being in love... always looking forward
to the next meeting with desire and trepidation...It's the
roller-coaster of love—up one day and down the next—no
two classes the same.
> Jane Tompkins, *A Life in School* 144–145

The procedure for accepting each fall's class of returning
students—those we call McBride Scholars at Bryn Mawr—is more
open than that for regular undergraduates. Crucial in the process
is the question of motivation; the McBride Admissions Committee
looks for and each fall finds about fifteen women who are eager to
apply themselves to study. In 1991, I began teaching a year-long
introductory course in composition and literature to a class of
McBrides and have continued most years since to offer some
variation of that course.

The friendships I have developed with many of the McBrides
have been the most satisfying aspect of my teaching career, if also

the source of some of its most demanding challenges. I have found it exhilarating and exhausting to work with these women who come to Bryn Mawr so certain that the education we offer here is important. The McBrides stretch and challenge themselves, one another, and me, in ways none of us have been challenged before, and I am deeply and often difficultly entangled in the dynamics of their absorption with learning.

Like all the other engagements in teaching and learning recounted in this book, my work with the McBrides oscillates among multiple points, including the affective investments each of us brings to our classes and the structural arrangements that both limit and enable our work together. In trying to make sense of this complex, ever-changing dynamic, I have drawn on a range of resources. Particularly useful has been Shoshana Felman's essay, "Psychoanalysis and Education" and Hannah Arendt's work, "Philosophy and Politics." I have taken additional help from a number of interpreters of Arendt's work, including Aaron Schutz, Anne Ruggles Gere and Susan Bickford. But I have been most helped to understanding by the McBrides themselves.

At the end of the first-year writing course, I often assign Paulo Freire's *Pedagogy of the Oppressed* and ask each of the McBrides to write, as a summary project for the class, her own "pedagogy of a student." I draw below on a range of responses to that request as well as a few others gathered in other assignments or from electronic communications. Although I have solicited, selected, and arranged these essays and intersperse them with commentary, I do not see them as contained or finally explained by what others or even each other have to say. Because I hear them sounding simultaneously, it has even been difficult for me to organize them sequentially. Choosing an order for presentation implies a certain trajectory, which may both do violence to the integrity of individual essays and give the impression that later ones correct those that come earlier in the sequence.

In searching for an appropriate structure for this chapter, I have been haunted by the voice of Andrea Miller, who finally, frankly, said to me, "I do not want to play the role you have assigned me in this narrative of your education as a teacher." The essays I offer here have shaped my learning; their arrangement is, of course, also shaped by what I have learned. I present them as a cacophony of voices circling around several points: the passion the McBrides bring into our conferences and classes, the anxieties that our engagements here generate and the ways that our educational structures both impede and enable them to get what they have come here for—as well as a few matters they may not have been seeking, an education they may not have imagined.

On First Falling in Love
Pedagogy of the Starry-Eyed Mother. English 016. Bryn Mawr College.
Spring 1993

Each and every morning that I set off to go to school, I first drop off my little daughter, aged two and a half, at day care. Each and every morning she protests my leaving, by crying, sobbing, wailing (what word describes a child's cry for her mother?). I want to tell her that leaving her is just as hard for me. It is, in fact, a wrenching, a tearing, a gaping wound that does not close up until I am holding her in my arms again at the end of the day. Even then, it never closes up entirely and threatens to reopen and bleed at any sign that she is unhappy.

Despite this though, I happily, eagerly, walk off to catch my train, to begin my journey to the singular world of academia. In my eagerness is there something of a woman running away from her family to a clandestine meeting with an illicit lover? That is how it seems to me sometimes. I am so attached to this process of "getting an education" and so pleased to spend time in the physical embodiment of this process, the Gothic buildings, the manicured grounds, the book-lined corridors of this school, Bryn Mawr. I find that I am on the same roller-coaster ride of attraction and repulsion, elation and despair, juggling feelings of security and rejection, as I would experience if I were living through an episode of romantic love.

Is it a necessary condition of a love affair to have a fantasy picture of one's lover? If so, I certainly have one. My fantasy picture of Bryn Mawr College is of a cloistered, sheltered place, devoted to the development of women's minds—a place to study, to learn, to contemplate, a retreat from the physical demands of raising a child, of house-keeping.

My fantasy also encompasses the professors. They seem to me to be supreme beings, much more erudite and scholarly than I could ever hope to be. I want to be like them and know everything they know. I want them to share their minds, impart their knowledge and skills, and regard me worthy of their endeavor. Their assessments are often responsible for those horrible plunges from joy to despondency. My attraction for academia takes the form of a longing, almost a physical desire.

Roberta Baer-Schimmel. Note to Anne, with a late paper
I love you: your compassion, understanding, friendship. It helps me believe in myself!

Mary Green. Note to Anne, preparatory to a conference
I have been afraid of what I perceive to be your capacity to unintentionally hurt me. Admittedly, I could be responding to my sense of your "presence," so that who you are may have very little to do with how I feel. One thing that needs to happen in my conversations with you is to discover the source of the fear on my part, and to reveal that to you and make you aware of what it is that generates such feelings in a student like me.

Anne
In "Psychoanalysis and Education," Shoshana Felman calls attention to the process of transference that occurs for many students in the classroom. Following Freud's argument that later acquaintances take over the emotional heritage of our parental relations and so encounter sympathies and antipathies to which they haven't contributed, Felman suggests that teachers commonly function for their students as substitute—and of course profoundly ambivalent—Oedipal figures (29). But if transference, the compulsive unconscious reproduction of an archaic emotional pattern, is an inevitable experience for many students (see also Kelly 132), what happens simultaneously to their teachers, who occupy the position of authority in this dynamic? What difference does it make when both the teacher and the students are women of a certain age?

And what difference does it make when the framework for our engagement is a first-year writing class, the exemplar for the sort of intimate, personalized pedagogy on which Bryn Mawr prides itself? The first-year composition course here involves half-hour conferences, every other week, with individual students, to discuss their even-more-frequent writing assignments. Many of the McBrides come to those assignments, to the conferences in which they are discussed and to the classes in which they are presented with enormous hopes and as-enormous fears: often they worry that they are not good enough to be here, not able to do the work required. In our conferences, I try to calm such anxieties, offering lots of encouragement along with whatever constructive criticism seems useful. I have long been convinced that such private conversations, which enable both me and the student to focus entirely on her individual work, are the center of the success of this first-year course as an introduction to college-level thinking and writing.

A few years ago, however, a colleague who came to Bryn Mawr from New York University gave me occasion to re-think this assessment by reflecting on the different sorts of spaces in which we might meet with our students and the kinds of conversations those differing spaces might engender. Anne Horn suggested that the far-more casual, open, catch-as-catch-can tutoring that takes place in the hallways at NYU, where graduate teaching assistants don't have private offices, sends a message to students that writing is a public act, openly discussable, easily revisable. She hypothesized that Bryn Mawr's conferences, regularly scheduled in the uninterrupted seclusion of our private offices, might have a very different effect on our students' sense of what writing is about and how it is done: it may become an anxious private act.

In a *College English* article, Aaron Schutz and Anne Ruggles Gere posit a similar comparison and expand on its possibilities. They explore the ways in which private writing conferences such as we offer at Bryn Mawr might work to inhibit not just the exploratory act of writing but the more public work of the classroom, and beyond:

> Tutoring has limited capacity to dislodge...individualistic and meritocratic visions of success and failure...This limitation can be traced to...a *tendency* of the tutoring context ...The essentially "private" nature of tutoring poses problems for a pedagogy that seeks more "public" ends. (136, 142)

Drawing on Arendt's distinction between private and public modes of interaction, Schutz and Gere argue that private "practices involve unique relations between pairs of individuals where one 'cares' for another, while 'public' relations involve collective relations between multiple individuals who join together in a common project" (132). They suggest that classrooms "might productively be re-conceptualized as potential 'publics'...[in which] individuals retain their points of view as they work together on common projects...an alternative to the 'private' personal growth perspective" (141).

Schutz and Gere are helping me re-think the ways in which both my conferences and my classrooms might function not only as occasions for individual development but also as forums in which common projects are undertaken. I am restive, however, with their (and Arendt's) strict separation between private and public experience. Unacknowledged by their binary formulation is the dynamic interpenetration of the two modes of interaction, the multiple ways in which supportive individual relations may contribute to collective projects, and its converse: the social construction of personal identity. Each McBride comes to Bryn Mawr in search of a certain sort of education, hoping to meet certain needs of her own. In doing so, she enters an insistently social process, which uncovers new aspects of self, generates a range of new anxieties.

On What Arises...

Pedagogy of the Confused. English 016. Bryn Mawr College. Spring 1993

I suppose I thought to become educated would be an act of defining myself. I could say, "I am an educated person. Respect me. Accept me. Allow me to enter into your group. I am not satisfied being who I am. I want to be part of the group who is more privileged, and I want more options for myself."

But instead of getting close to being able to define myself as educated, I went in the opposite direction. I became utterly confused, and all my defenses fell by the wayside. And what emerged were my emotions. I feel so angry about this—like a two-year-old who is given a red lollipop when she wanted a purple one. I didn't get the kind of education I wanted. I didn't expect to learn about myself. This part of my Bryn Mawr education will take a while for me to digest.

I'm starting to see other ways of becoming educated: knowing, seeing, thinking, becoming aware of something today that you didn't know, see, think, or were aware of yesterday. The most important thing is to experience movement and growth. That makes me think of the women staring out of the windows in Sandra Cisneros's stories. And that makes me sad. It's better to be angry, even angry with oneself maybe, than to sit passively and stare out of the window.

Maybe a Bryn Mawr Education isn't for everyone, but everyone who needs a good shaking up should experience English 015–016 at Bryn Mawr. I could just picture those women who sit looking out of windows sitting in Anne's class. I can picture these women so well, you see, because I *used* to be one of those women myself.

Coming from a severely shamed-based childhood, my antennae are constantly searching out any vibrations that could be injurious to me. It's an art that's been perfected over a lifetime and one that is difficult to ignore. At the same time though, it enables me to be hypersensitive to others, their fears and their needs. I became acutely aware of this as I listened to the dialogue between my classmates.

I was astounded by the ease, confidence, and clarity in which my classmates expressed their criticism and view of our assignments. I became excited and validated when my thoughts paralleled theirs. Ideas and thoughts filled my head, wanting to explode onto the center of the table. But my fear of embarrassment, of my views being inferior, of sounding stupid, prevented me from sharing my thoughts. I felt locked behind a steel door that the years had rusted shut.

As the year drew to a close, I began to feel a connection with others growing, and with it came a feeling of their acceptance of me. To a few, I shared my feelings of inadequacy, and in return I got their understanding.

What have I learned? I've learned to trust others as well as myself. I've learned to accept my limitations.

Education and Me. English 016. Bryn Mawr College. Spring 1993.

I will try to answer in this paper the question you asked me in conference on Tuesday, April 20, 1993: "How could I have helped you?" I am not sure that I could have been helped by you until I learned the language of education. Since I entered Bryn Mawr I have faced some very deep-seated fears. They are so ingrained in me that I do not know what they are.

This year I proved to myself that I can learn how to write. I am on the first step of the ladder of critical thinking and analysis. I am able to speak more clearly, to follow conversations. I feel like a fog in my brain has been cleared. I am able to listen to other people's views, ask them questions.

I do not know if it was possible for you to help me any more than you did. I confronted my deep-seated fears on education and conquered some of them. The one thing I did was not run and quit like I wanted to. I feel that this was worth the experience because I have to exorcise the ghosts of the past.

Myra Reichel. Pedagogy of the Would-Be Student

She arrives with her heart in her mouth and butterflies in her stomach. Presented with a laudable teacher, she enters the hornet's nest of education. Feeling not worth a straw, she is afraid to be discovered as the pseudo-student that she is. She has always known that she falls short in the meritorious application of herself. She struggles to be reliable in her grades, performs inadequately on tests, and fails to speak with significance at the proper moments.

Suddenly, she finds herself flustered, tormented, and caught in a boot camp of academic survival. The worst has happened. She has met the enemy, her own sense of self built on paltry footings. Rapidly her valueless position causes her to retreat, grieving, into a wrapper of distraught heartache. She suffers a laceration to her ego. This shock cuts her to the quick, forces her back into the fray to prove herself worthy. She tussles with her binding, comes loose by tugging at her heart strings, and discovers under the rubble years of mortification.

She collapses by slip-sliding into a fear of success and sets out to prove herself a sham. She laments her inability to show her real character. She denies profiting by her creditable work, holding all that she does to be inadequate. Her futile attempts only weaken her position.

She hasn't a prayer that she will be able to redeem herself. She hopes by supplicating herself to the integrity of her teacher that she will be found deserving. Her apprehension causes her to be tied up in knots at the final hours. Coming to grips with her horror of gaining a position at the expense of fellow students, she sets out to keep herself from going to the dogs. Coming out of her cocoon, she presents herself in her own sphere, risking her true self. A year has gone by and she has gone so far. At this point in time, can she do more than act on who she is and what she knows?

Anne

"Who she is and what she knows" are emphatically in transition for the McBrides: challenged, defined and re-defined by the focused speaking and attentive listening that occur in our conferences and classrooms. That this interactive process is decidedly unpredictable is one of the themes of the political philosopher Susan Bickford, who studies the role that "focused awareness," "being mindful or observant" plays in "the process of public problem solving" (2, 41). Bickford is interested in listening attention as an activity of citizenship, but her line of inquiry seems to me also wonderfully descriptive of the educational work that goes on in sites such as Bryn Mawr:

> Speaking and listening...have a spontaneous quality...We have the capacity to hear something about the world differently through the

sounding of another's perspective; we are able to be surprised by others and by our own selves...the field of meaning is itself expanded, recast. (162)

Bickford's analysis of these interactive dynamics has convinced me that such unpredictability is not only unavoidable but highly desirable. She draws heavily on Arendt's insights to demonstrate how our differences from one another both call us into speech and prevent us from controlling how we are understood:

> It is our distinctiveness that creates the need for our own voice to sound through...We would not need...a space in which to speak to each other, if each of us were not distinct...[But] we are active and unpredictable in listening as well as speaking...It is tempting to see...a struggle...to appear as who I think I am, to be heard as who I want to be...there is an implicit desire for mastery...But...no individual can simply impose her or his will on another and insist on being heard in a particular way...others' reactions to me are themselves actions, unpredictable and novel. This is the paradox of public appearance: our very appearance as an active unique "who" relies on the attention of active others whose perceptions we do not control. If we acknowledge those with whom we are acting as capable of judgment...being heard differently than we want to be...is an unavoidable...possibility. (58, 129–130)

Bickford's work has helped me re-trace and understand the structured spontaneity that constitutes both my classrooms and individual student conferences. The college has established these spaces; I construct designs within them; my students and I each enter them with certain purposeful intentions. Yet we as often discover there, in conversation, things about ourselves and one another that we never imagined.

On The Unpredictability of Structures
Jeanne-Rachel Salomon. Pedagogy of the Stuffed Goose

There I was in Anne Dalke's class, and there came the heat, the steam, and the smell of the loveliest herbs! It didn't take long and I felt like a French goose, caged in a wooden, boxy device, especially and ingeniously invented for just this barbaric purpose: force-feeding to produce the coveted foie gras. No choice for either goose or me but to endure the torture, yet neither her stomach nor my brain made were capable of processing what was just too much to digest. A goose responds to such treatment with a sick, enlarged liver—I did with a highly energized yet fragmented brain. I can't speak for the poor goose, since I'm not too familiar with its metabolism, but I am expertly familiar with mine: I was drugged. The firework of sparkling ideas when millions of synapses connected while reading or talking or thinking about Michel Foucault or Stephen Gould or Renato Rosaldo or Fritjof Capra; the associations which these sparks brought out, the memories they called up put me on high and no time to let all this sink in, or store or deal with, because the next text had to be read, the next paper had to be written—the whole exercise just a firework and all the exciting sparkles lost, extinguished.

Jeanne-Rachel Salomon. Notes to Anne

I want to thank you for your midwifery work!

It is said that biography becomes biology: the intense labor you put in and the merriment you create in class will all be part of my very cells.

I think of the sum of your teaching as nutrients which nourished my soul and thus my spirit and body into health. The nutrients cannot be traced—they transformed, but the beauty of the healthy organism is proof of their intake.

Thank you for guiding me patiently and with lots of humour and understanding through the dangers of testimony/confession, enthusiasm/despair, loneliness/loquacity.

You displayed the psychologist's virtue of non-reciprocality as the patient—being sick—is allowed to be unreasonable, even accusative, while the therapist refrains from reacting in kind. I thank you for your therapist's understanding—I learned from all my mistakes!

Andrea Miller. E-mail

Have you ever noticed how the medical profession creates an unequal yoke between physician and patient? Picture a physician entering an exam room, closing the door to the world outside.

Here sits a patient, who comes to him for answers and help. He listens attentively to her concerns. Her words are intimate and serious. It is her life and vitality she entrusts to him. Then because of who he is, he reaches beyond empathy into action. He takes his commitment to her well-being seriously. Then takes his leave and on to another room to do just the same for another person. And another after that, and so on.

Careful orchestration prevents a patient from seeing the doctor with anyone but herself. To the patient, it could easily feel like a monogamous relationship and a fulfilling one at that. From her viewpoint, who else gives her such careful attention, never dismisses problems as trivial or ignores a complaint? There is nothing and no one competing for her attention in that exam room, a condition that is unlikely to be equaled in any other daily contact. It is understood that the office visit is a construction and not spontaneous interaction. Nevertheless, it is still enticing for her to become emotionally trapped in a one-way attachment for her doctor because of the conditions superimposed on an office visit.

Of course, most adults play a good game of reason over emotion, saying, "Dr. So-and-so, I'm sure you don't remember me from your many patients, but..." Don't fool yourself, patient, we all inwardly would love nothing better than to be the one that stands out in the doctor's mind. The remembered one. The significant one. It's because the doctor means so much to us, we inwardly long to mean something to him.

I might easily dismiss the irrational attachment people have for those like doctors in positions of authority mixed with service. And yet that is precisely my position to you—as teacher, it is understood that you will freely expose my infant thoughts, you are entitled to draw open the drawers of my memory, shine a light into my shadowy subconscious—you have the authority to work over my raw and unfinished thoughts, dismantling them and piecing them back together. Yes, I pour it all out in my papers, lay myself bare for your attentive going over. That sweet pain of exposure yields fruit: you show me how to reshape my thoughts, redirect my ideas. And then you test their strength. Sometimes they are broken in the crucible. Other times they are made stronger, surer. You are my trainer, quickening my mind, burning the waste, and making me strong.

To that end, you give me focused, singular attention—like the physician. Our time together in conference is solely for my use and benefit, and sometimes I feel a flush come over me, for my intimate thoughts to be so bare on the exam table before you— never mind that it is your job to search and assess and that you do this for sixteen students at a time—it makes no earthly difference. My mind tells me that you are like a good physician, going from room to room, and I should accept the inequality. But it is no use. Herein is the frustration of one-way relationships: You are the single most important influence on what matters most to me—my mind and writing, and I am but one of your many students.

I do so want to please you (sometimes, I even want to become you!). I guess I accept (resign?) myself to the realization that the point at which you and I converge is a classroom, you the teacher, I the student. It is useful. But there will come a time when I will have to grow beyond that and think for myself. I suppose the great difficulty for me is that I am your student, and the way we interact is based on the dictates of that kind of relationship. No matter what you think of me, I am "a student" ("a specimen," a la Walker Percy, maybe a fine specimen, but still ...)

This week after class was the first time I was able to have a productive discussion about the reading material with classmates outside of class. Why? Maybe because we are finally getting to know/trust each other. I sense that you want the balance of power in class to equalize—or at least you are looking for ways to deal with that tension, and I think that this is a step.

Anne

Yes, Andrea, I am wishing (and working) to equalize what you call the balance of power in the classroom: I invite silent students to speak, talky students to listen. But your story reminds me that when I was a student myself, I was often—usually— disappointed by the other students, impatient with their stumblings in our classes. I much preferred to hear what the professors had to say. (I'm not sure why my own teaching has since become so student centered, so focused on figuring out what you all want—unless, as my colleague Kaye Edwards suggests, I'm trying still to reach myself-as-student, who's alive and looking for someone to talk to.)

Another story may help to explain why your conferences with me so often seemed like visits to the doctor's office—and why, like the physician you describe, I can't forget the other students waiting outside the door.

On the night before Easter 1981—late, too late—I got a phone call. My younger brother Chip had been in a car accident. He was not conscious. The next call came early Easter morning. He was not responsive. I called again. The nurse, who knew me from home, said, "Anne, I don't think he's going to make it."

I went to my husband, who was caring for our daughter. Standing beside her changing table, looking out the window—this was a West Philadelphia row house, we could not look far out—looking at her, not looking at him, I whispered, "I'm afraid he's going to die." Jeff said, "He can't die. He won't die." He said this with certainty, and I took comfort from his assurance. So when I got the next call, I couldn't understand what I was hearing. I asked, dumbly, "Is he DEAD?" My mother, dully: "Oh, yes. He is dead."

This is (certainly one reason) why I teach the way I do—because once I was comforted by that which was not true, by a comfort that turned out to be no comfort at all. "He can't die." Oh, yes, he could. I think that, in my teaching, I refuse such false comfort, am impelled by the hope that I will not be surprised again, by facts I do not have. (Or facts I have but am not willing to face. Facts others have but will not speak. Chip was dead when I spoke with the nurse. But she did not think she should be the one to tell me.)

Kaye Edwards also figured this one out for me. At the end of the first semester we taught together, she suggested that we go 'round, ask our students to say something about what they had gotten out of the course, what they have learned, what they have found useful. I said, "No. Maybe they did not find it useful. Maybe they did not like it. We will not be hearing the truth."

She was just looking to end the course on an affirmative note. But I was after the truth, the elusiveness of which impels me—

perhaps, as Andrea says, like a physician—in the searches I conduct both in my classes and in student conferences. That is the cause of my questioning, unremitting, my refusal of complacency, my insistence that, hard and deep as we may dig, we will never, ever get to the bottom.

My brother was not the first young man I knew to die. Robert Sanderson and Al Lampert were fellow graduate students, both my good friends. Robert was mountain climbing, August 1978; he did not attach his safety rope. Al fell asleep, January 1981, and did not wake up. Chip was drinking, driving, April 1981, when he wrecked his car.

I tried to make sense of these deaths: if they were purely accidental, I could not bear it. I could bear it less, if they had causes. A friend sent me an essay by William Sloane Coffin, about the death of his son, also a careless driver. Refusing the comfort of neighbors, who said this was God's will, Coffin insisted, "God's heart was the first of all hearts to break" when the car went into Boston Harbor that night (30).

His response opened the way to my search for a God who can keep us company. And it opened the way back into my classes, as places where we, and the texts, are also keeping one another company as we look together for understanding.

But with such difficulty!

On The Company We Keep
Minna Canton Duchovnay. The Pedagogy of the Spider

At the end of the first semester I thought of our 015 course as a spider's web. The spider represented all of us with our many ideas and our discussion. We drew out the silken threads; we jumped to many places to form the web, weaving crisscrossed strands. Thus the structure of the web—its shape and size—depended on the breadth and diversity of our ideas. In the first semester the shape of the web seemed many sided and beautifully drawn.

During the second semester I thought that the web has not described so wide an area as it did in the first semester. Or perhaps the web has become misshapen. Sometimes there seemed to be less variety in the discussion. Often there was less nuance, less divergence than I would have liked. The discussions did not seem so multifaceted, nor did they build a web in as interesting a shape as in the months before.

But how could that have happened?

I have concluded that I may have depended too much on the others for their understanding of what we were reading. I needed the class to tell me what they thought, so I could understand better what I thought, but my impatience to understand is ever present. I want to understand, to know, before I have even learned.

To hear myself speak out about ideas before I barely grasped the concepts helped me formulate what I thought I understood!

What I wish from this experience at Bryn Mawr is to compete with myself, not others; to develop patience for letting myself learn what I do, cannot seem to understand; to read and re-read until I can tell the story behind the theory...

I hope that I can be my own spider building a bigger web, seeking out new ideas and new discussions, starting from a center I can claim for myself, reaching for the edges of the web ever more broadly to spin a structure of knowledge and understanding. The question remains: can I let myself build a structure whose shape I cannot predict?

Patricia Scott. Reflections

Spending an entire year with one group of people has been both a challenge and a delight, not too different from being a part of a family. There was changing and reshaping of our original group. One person perhaps did not feel a part of our class and decided to leave Bryn Mawr. One woman decided that she did not need us, that she was ready to approach the outer scholastic world without this communal rite of passage. And one student became ill and was forced to leave our niche. I mourned them all. I do not accept loss or embrace change easily. We have been like sisters together with one mother who has striven to nurture us towards growth. And, like sisters, we both encouraged and competed with each other in the process.

Unbeknown to me, I selected the class section that thrived on difference. Although all female, our group comprised vast ethnic, social, sexual, religious, political, and philosophical diversity. It was inevitable that there would be differences of opinion. Anne has expressed that she would have liked even more opposition in order to stimulate interesting discussion. For me, the frequent tension was enough to challenge my Libra nature. In my own family, I have always been the peacemaker, the middle person who smoothes the hurts and disagreements. I confess that I am most comfortable when people get along with each other. Having no entitlement to a peacemaker role in this group, however, I was forced to endure the dissension that by nature I have always tended to resist.

In sitting through the disagreements during our class discussions, I learned that it is not conflict *per se* that bothers me. In fact, friction and contrast can be exciting spices in any group dynamics. What irks me is the manner in which we often hinder the dialogue toward understanding during any conflict. One day in class, I was surprised when my stifled voice of anger erupted to protest the way in which we handled differences during a heated class debate. How can we passionately disagree while still respecting one another? Are we all merely walking wounded soldiers reacting to old injuries from our own personal lives? Perhaps that is why we often react to difference with immediate anger to attack or defend. I am not calling for us to stifle our truths, to blend or compromise or seek agreement. I respect directness, honesty, and fervor. I wish only that we could seek first to understand before we react, to investigate before we prosecute. It is quick anger with a dagger that concerns me.

I think the family of our class is a microcosm for the world at large. We see the world through different lenses, because we have emerged from various contexts. And yet we are sisters, not enemies. There is no war here, except the private battles with our individual souls.

Deborah Kocsis. "Warm Fuzzies," "Cold Pricklies," and Turtles

My brother familiarized my family with the terms "warm fuzzies" and "cold pricklies" when he was about four years old. He came home from nursery school one day announcing that he had learned about good feelings and bad ones. This year I became aware of "turtles" as a metaphor for questions ("turtles all the way down"). English 015/016 has been a year of "warm fuzzies," "cold pricklies" and turtles.

While "turtles" have been in my mind since our first class meeting, I had long since forgotten about "warm fuzzies" and "cold pricklies." However, I was recently reminded of them during a few of our class discussions. Our class frequently became involved in heated discussions. In one particular discussion, people on all sides ended feeling either hurt, angry, frustrated, or some combination of the three. The specific discussion I have in mind turned into a debate about the proper tone and language for a discussion.

This debate subsequently seemed to deteriorate into a quest for "warm fuzzies," some in the class questioning attitude and the use of body language and others questioning the issues of self-censorship. In this search for a language that would be palatable for all, "warm fuzzies," "cold pricklies" seemed to come over the room. These "cold pricklies" from what I gather took as many forms as there were people who had them, from anger to sadness to withdrawal. I personally fell into the withdrawal category.

It became apparent to me during the next class that I was not the only one who had this wish. The discussion that next week was very quiet, even-tempered, and pleasant. It seemed to me however to be too pleasant, too innocuous. Although I was relieved that the tension level was down from the previous week, I was disappointed that the discussion was not very stimulating: there was no edge, no excitement, to it.

Learning to think critically and articulate my ideas was a goal I had upon entering this class. I have a tendency to not want to say things—to censor myself—for fear of offending others and I had hoped to overcome this fear in English 015/016. These particular discussions, these searches for "warm fuzzies," have again made me reluctant to speak, especially regarding controversial topics. "Warm fuzzies," both as the means and the end, seem to hinder honest, revealing discussion. I feel somewhat cheated by what I do not say and what I feel others may be holding back. Perhaps "warm fuzzies" and "cold pricklies" should be left in nursery school classrooms. I know I would prefer to learn what a classmate really thinks or feels than to have "warm fuzzies" all the time: warm fuzzies can get in the way of a good "turtle" hunt.

Nancy Schmucker. Listening: The Lesson at the Big Table in the Center of the Porch

My fellow McBrides and I met for two hours each week, each of us bringing our unique personal histories to the big table in the center of the porch. All of us searching. Our time was spent in discussion. It was not easy, nor was it always pleasant. For me, the big table was the place where I began to listen.

I was always frustrated by this class, overwhelmed by the amount of material and all the new ideas. I never felt capable of grasping deeper nuances. I shrank in fear. My thoughts seemed shallow. My writing was pained and forced, the discussions difficult. My input seemed vague and wandering. I felt disconnected. The blank stares indicated that my slant was nonsensical. I felt like a seashell, emitting faint sounds of an inner world I was unable to explain.

I wondered if my classmates understood that I was attempting to work my thoughts, ideas, and philosophies out through them. I never began a contribution to a discussion knowing what my point would be. I depended on them to help me refine my thoughts. My life has been my education, pieces of information gathered over thirty years yet unexplored. I now endeavor to connect these pieces through formal education. Did my classmates understand that? Did they hear my call?

More important, did I hear my classmates? Until this year, I never knew what it meant to *listen*. I never heard words on a page, the conviction of a voice, the tone of a text. I never made an effort. Now I listen intently, searching words for definition and meaning, eyes for belief and passion; asking questions in an effort to gain better understanding; focusing attention; thinking about the connections and differences between ideas and philosophies.

I came to this place in search of my voice and intellect, hoping to make a contribution. I now realize that in order to achieve these goals I must listen more intently than I ever imagined. I must listen to everything. I am on fire. So much to think about and explore. So much to listen to.

Kathy Barnes. Talking Like a Man, Going Ape, and Bryn Mawr: Finishing College at Forty-Eight

There is something important that I have forgotten. It's a yearning voice that I'm not sure about—something of my own, nearly silent, unspoken for so long—a ghost of a whisper now. I start listening until I listen all the time. I can't hear anything else. I quit my job, come to the Castle Bryn Mawr and begin the climb, up the tower, spiraling up, to ever smaller enclosures.

At the end of my interview, McBride Dean Jean Wu says something that suddenly sells me: "You will find some kindred spirits here." That is all I need to hear; I had no idea before she said it—like touching a sore spot that I didn't know was there. Three months later, I am sitting in a room full of windows, squeezed in tight around a big seminar table. Everyone is dressed differently—some in what I think of as work clothes: skirts and blouses, a colorful scarf around the neck. Others like me in jeans; the professor, Anne, is wearing a T-shirt with turtles on the front and a denim skirt. We have already been to orientation, so we've seen each other before today, said our names and what brought us to college at anywhere from twenty-four to nearly sixty years old. I told them I'm here because my father died and left me money, because I know that my career has pushed, stretched, and shaped me as much as it's going to; I have reached my limits after eighteen years of nursing. I have a sense that each person has an interesting story to tell; we represent a kaleidoscope of back-grounds, reasons for being here—some of us have in common perhaps only that we are here together—at the first class at Bryn Mawr, with (more or less) time having passed since high school. I hope there may be, among them, one or two kindred spirits, but it's too early to tell.

So, the first day of school, there are seventeen of us McBrides, each with an opinion to share. Many are speaking, in turn, politely, some more cautious, and some more bold, than others. We're having an animated discussion about women's education. But the conversation slides more and more into (what I think of as knee-jerk) agreement with each other—sugar sweet, aren't we nice. Suddenly, words fairly lurch out of my mouth, a little too loud, from somewhere deep inside: "I didn't come here to learn about emotion! I already know about that. I came here to learn to talk like a man!" I punctuate by slamming an open hand down on the table. The group is silent for a heartbeat or two but then springs into a tumult of disagreement, even outrage. But the class is over. I am a bit stunned. I have said something without thinking that sounds appalling; intuitively I know it's not exactly what I mean, but I don't really know where my statement is coming from; right now, I only fear their judgment. What am I doing here?

Anytime, the few times, I have written something, I have been filled with anxiety, my insides exposed to the world. What is it about the written word? Does it frighten me to say things I can't take back, that will be judged in ways I can't predict or control? Is it the power of the words that I don't feel is mine to wield? Or is it my own power that the words will reveal, that I have no right to?

I write in my journal to stay alive, as an escape valve for the pressure cooker of my internal life. I write out of desperation in the middle of the night, unable to sleep because my mind is racing. I write when the top of my head is flying off, my gut is burning. I write so I won't self-destruct by spontaneous combustion. I do have something to say — the words live deep inside in a special place. My strongest desire is to touch my most inner feelings — to stroke and soothe them — to explore this place of secrets instead of screwing the windows and doors down so tight the words are only forced out, squeezed through cracks. I want to do this — make love to them, kiss them tenderly, dress them up and strut them around — to enter my own house and become myself for a while.

Going back to college, even at forty-four years old, it was as if I were eighteen again, words flying out when I least expected them, again and again. When I came to the McBride program, I disconnected from the safety of a known identity — I lost friends, and relationships with my family changed. I have felt like a child, starting the search for identity all over at times with a similar sense of anxiety, disorientation, and confusion. I found myself fundamentally re-evaluating who I am, questioning my role, my aloneness and mortality. That first McBride class, English 015–016, began a process of self-discovery through reading and discussing literature that has persisted through the last four years. Many of the books we read spoke to me, words diving down deep, bringing up ideas and feelings, giving me emotional-intellectual tools with which to work.

I am standing in the doorway looking in. Professor Beard, working at her computer, turns her beaming light my way: "Hello! Come in, sit down!" her musical voice greets me with warm enthusiasm. I go to her office to tell her that I am having trouble writing my paper and why. She just sits and listens, but she listens hard with her hands folded in her lap. After I stop talking she continues to listen, long enough for my heart to open up even more. I start again, going a bit deeper into my dilemma; tears sprout in my eyes but do not fall. And then she speaks. She says exactly what I need to hear. I don't know how she does it, but she does. We talk about writing; our conversation occurs on a deeper level than I am used to with someone I have recently met, because she is comfortable there.

I *have* found kindred spirits here at Bryn Mawr, among my fellow McBrides. Just as I originally suspected, they all have stories to tell—lives full of conflict like my own. They are women who have not given up but are still struggling, actively seeking to fulfill their dreams, being here, at this challenging, demanding school. I've made close friends who have shared their life stories with me as I have with them. Friendships that I hope will go on long after Bryn Mawr is a memory. I have also watched "traditional age undergrads" each year coming more into focus, blossoming before my eyes, beginning to gel into mature adults brimming with promise. How moved I was the first time I noticed that we were going through similar identity crises.

I go to see Professor Beard again. I come in thinking that I am here to pick up a paper and to catch up with a chat. But before many sentences are out, I realize that I have come to her with a deeply felt crisis of confidence. I have lost faith in myself altogether. "I am just barely beginning to find my voice. I'm wondering if I have anything worth saying." I tell her I'm not ready to leave this place that I have loved so much. She says to just look at the comments on my paper. She has written only a couple of sentences, eloquent heartfelt words that reach in and touch me in that innermost place where I live—words that are directly addressed to my fears, though she had written them months before. I fill up with gratitude and relief, my hope renewed.

Emerson wrote that "we but half express ourselves, and are ashamed of that divine idea which each of us represents." One of the principal reasons I came to Bryn Mawr was to discover (evolve) a new form of self-expression. I felt that I had not developed any means for articulating large parts of myself—I could "but half express" myself. As I come into my own voice, and at the same time become more connected to the "divine" spirit within me, I often feel overwhelmed, as if I am not equipped to handle this, being so alive.

Exterior. Thomas Hall. Bryn Mawr College.
Photograph by Carlos Garcia. 2001.

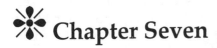 # Chapter Seven

"Fullness of Life": Class as Paradise

Why couldn't they see that this was the earthly paradise?
The course was what all the theory and criticisms of
literature was pointing toward, had hoped someday could
be achieved. Why couldn't they understand that we're just
like the barrier island, the ribbon of sand, that's always
being created and destroyed, always changing, ever the
same? ...I cling to the metaphor of the barrier island,
which tells us not to cling.

Jane Tompkins, A Life in School 179–180

When the ocean heaves sending rhythms of water ashore,
Piedade looks to see what has come. Another ship,
perhaps, but different, heading to port, crew and
passengers, lost and saved, atremble, for they have been
disconsolate for some time. Now they will rest before
shouldering the endless work they were created to do
down here in Paradise.

Toni Morrison, Paradise 318

In her most recent novel, Toni Morrison gives an account of two
communities—two attempts at creating Paradise on earth—which
are unable to exist side by side: the presence of a nearby convent
inhabited by "lost" women is seen as a threat and destroyed by
the founders of the black town of Haven. The novel ends with a
profound questioning of the impulse which impelled that act:
"How exquisitely human was the wish for permanent happiness,

and how thin human imagination became trying to achieve it"
(306). "How could so clean and blessed a mission devour itself
and become the world they had escaped?" (292). How, one of the
town founders asks himself, could he have "become what the Old
Fathers cursed: the kind of man who set himself up to judge, rout
and even destroy the needy, the defenseless, the different?" (302)

The dynamic that Morrison gives fictional form in Oklahoma
in the 1970s also plays itself out, over and over again, in our
American college classrooms at the beginning of the twenty-first
century. Jane Tompkins plaintively describes how the
conversations held in such spaces tend towards righteous
judgment:

> I thought we could sidestep the need to measure and find fault, with
> ourselves or with the texts we read. I wanted to be safe, "safe from the
> wolf's black jaw and the dull ass's hoof...I'd been criticized too early in
> my life and for too long. Now I wanted to be free from judgments and
> from judging...But [my students] were still learning how to criticize.
> (176–177)

Sheryl O'Donnell offers an astute analysis of how-and-why
such professorial "dreams of safety" often fail in the classroom:
because they attempt to "domesticate" and deny the "radical
Otherness" of our students, who think of themselves as
autonomous and self-sufficient:

> I dream of this classroom as...a safe place where students can think out
> loud together. I forget that this dream, like all feminist utopias, is
> literary: pastoral in its laminated images of teachers and students at
> leisure, epic in its characterization of the feminist classroom as *locus
> amatis*, beloved place. The pleasures of imagining the feminist classroom
> as such a "haven in a heartless world" of traditional academic life are
> perhaps Victorian. And such dreams play upon Victorian fantasies of
> ideal maternity: plenitude, safety, enclosure, self-sufficiency...my
> fantasies of the feminist classroom as benign may deny students' images
> of themselves as radical Others. I domesticate them. Pastoral fantasies of
> the feminist classroom as privileged space are easy for me to construct,
> and thus all the more insidious, because I can trick myself into thinking
> that I am making political sense out of personal experience (always a
> feminist dictum). I live in a state whose "rural" qualities, like my
> feminist pastoral fantasies, are largely illusory, highly artificial, and

utterly ahistorical. The myth of self-sufficiency…is so strong that my students can hardly trade papers with each other in the classroom for fear that someone will steal their idea. Their suspicions of others, their unwillingness to respect their own ideas or to converse with each other, their seeming emotional stinginess…are based, I think, on an ideology of private property (including ideas) as sacred and of the coherent ego as autonomous…the dream of cheerful solidarity, of pastoral enclosure and possessive individualism, was hard to kill. (258–259, 271)

Postmodern pedagogical theorists have actually been rather effective in "killing" such dreams, through their unremitting examinations of the oppressive effects of judgment—not just of students, but of their "liberatory" teachers. Drawing on Foucault's analysis of the "will to truth," Jennifer Gore is the perhaps the most explicit of educators who have described the ways in which "our self-proclaimed emancipatory discourses can have dominating effects," how our "radical pedagogies can function as repressively as those we seek to surpass" (*The Struggle for Pedagogies* xii, 137).

In this essay, I take up a rather different task: interrogating the "mythical" qualities of the classroom that O'Donnell finds so "insidious," in hopes of renovating and recuperating that space. In response to Gore's call for greater reflexivity, a willingness to question our work as progressive educators (10–11), I offer here an account of the labor of my living, my teaching, and, most particularly, my own tendencies to passionate judgment as they are grounded in my Quaker beliefs and practices. Sobered by O'Donnell's and Gore's descriptions of the ways in which spaces created as havens can become disabling for those they are meant to succor, yet heartened by Morrison's and Tompkins's stories of the endless work needed to sustain Paradise, I tell a contrapuntal tale, both like-and-different from each of theirs.

Central to my story is the paradoxical concept of Paradise: that walled-in space (the Greek root, "*paradeisos*," means "enclosed park"), which is our imagined place of perfection. Parker Palmer says that "to teach is to create a space" (xi–xii). But the spaces in which we teach are always inherently limiting. We and our students struggle to imagine and create ideal places for learning; it is the paradox of the possibilities that the limits of our classrooms invite that I want to explore here. What is the meaning of being a teacher in these paradoxical places of spaciousness and limit, where we engage in continual movements of withdrawal and return, emptying and filling, affirmation and denial, engagement and detachment?

In the third chapter of this book, I argued with Abby Reed that no structure can accommodate the needs of all those who gather within it, that each re-formation will produce its own resistance. In the fourth chapter, I posited a counterclaim: that a faithful commitment to structure itself, an assurance that we will meet regularly and labor together—as well as a willingness to let go, not to be too intrusive—may provide the only opening we need. In this chapter, I want to explore the enormous ambitions I bring into such spaces, my hopes for all that might be realized there: anticipations that can be enabling but also destructive to the process of learning. I begin my analysis, therefore, with a series of questions about my ambitions as a teacher. My response to these queries, which were posed by one of my returning students, involves two dimensions. The first is an account of the Quaker practices that undergird the havens I try to create in my classrooms. The second is a consideration of the terms of my employment as a regular part-time faculty member. I hope to contribute to the ongoing conversation about the appropriate use of adjunct faculty by tracing here not only the difficulties such arrangements may generate but also some of their potential.

Paradise Lost

At the age of fifty, I am working part-time as a way of institutionalizing a complex spiritual and academic life: in a rhythmic—well, ofttimes awkward and unsteady—alternation of contemplation and activity, separation and return, as I move continuously between center and margin (sometimes uncertain which is which). I locate the authority I claim for my teaching as well as the humility with which I practice it in that movement.

I first chose part-time work because I was in the midst of having children, wanted to spend time with them, and was married to someone whose income enabled me to do so. Over the years, that part-time job grew into a slow-track career. I came to teach upper-level courses in the English Department, to direct senior theses, to co-ordinate the Feminist and Gender Studies program. I participated in panels advertising the college to prospective students, in faculty seminars on campus, and at teachers' conferences around the country. And yet, as time went on, as I became increasingly over-age for rank—since one certain corollary of part-time work is the absence of advancement—I felt increasingly marginalized on campus. As my age-mates got tenure, took positions of authority on committees for appointments or institutional priorities, I have found myself relatively powerless and increasingly frustrated by my inability to help shape the mission and vision of the college, much less the concrete particularities which embody that vision.

Why do I not look for another job? Surely, in part, from inertia and from fear that I will not find a better one elsewhere. Even more surely, as a colleague in a like arrangement reminded me, because there are multiple compensations for this sort of regular part-time work. My marginal position on campus and the freedom attendant on my lack of responsibility there give me far more control over the structure and shape of my days and far more flexibility in pursuing both on- and off-campus interests than is possible for my colleagues whose jobs involve full-time commitments. My constant iteration of my marginality as an academic has very clear boundaries: however powerless I may feel on campus, I bear considerable authority, by virtue of race and class, outside it. I have likely tolerated, perhaps even embraced, my on-campus marginality over these many years, because I possess a certain security in the larger world.

But I want to explore now the degree to which my rather problematic sense of marginality may influence the kind of teaching I do as I (perhaps) try to fulfill in the classroom desires not fulfillable elsewhere on campus or in academia. In my exploration, I am led by a report on Nietzsche's claim that ascetic ideals and practices are motivated

> by feelings of *ressentiment*, and are developed as a strategy by which the weak seek to overcome the strong. Specifically, they seek to infect them with life-denying values that compromise bold assertions of power and

at the same time ensure continued existence for even weak human beings, albeit in a minimal way. (Peter Van Ness, et al. *Asceticism* 590)

One of my returning students has posited that such a strategy of compensation motivates both her commitment to educational work and my own. In an e-mail message dated December 1996, Andrea Miller mused,

> I never spend less than twenty-five to thirty hours/week on this class—and it is not that I waste time; it's that to do what you ask of me requires that, and more. You (unknowingly? probably not deliberately) make your class a disproportionately large part of our knowledge base.
>
> Both this and the upcoming semester, you introduced the syllabus by saying something to the effect of "I know this is WAY too much reading, but...I'm giving it to you anyway." Some profs throw down the gauntlet with heavy workload, as if to say, "anyone who isn't man enough, or doesn't take the class seriously, get the hell out and don't waste my time." This is not you. You want us all to excel in this class. In fact, you want this class to shape the rest of our college career. I know that this seminar is required for all students and is intended to be a foundation of sorts, but you have taken the requirements of the class and evolved them even further. Why do you need this class to so entirely consume us? Allow me for the moment to take an Ozick-ian approach to understanding you. (Rely on my own experience to transform the other into something knowable.) I returned to school on a part-time basis under the premise that I was going to balance mommy-ing with schooling. Yet I know in my heart that for all my stated intentions, that premise was largely a pretext to win unconditioned sanction for what I am really after. I have closed the door to the conventional means of ascension on the ladder of success, and this has become an alternate route. Let me explain: I am giving full-time hours to part-time classes. In this way, I can appease my loved ones (and myself) by a legitimate claim that I have not forsaken my motherly calling; I can outdo everyone in class, thereby "proving" my worth—demonstrating that I COULD HAVE gone the traditional route and excelled, but chose not to; I have an out, if ever I need one—if I don't get that Ph.D. (or that teaching position, or whatever), I can console myself with the simple explanation that it's not that I couldn't do it, it's that I sacrificed my ambitions for family needs.

All of that was rather ugly. It's, of course, deliberately so, to prove a point. I don't hate myself or think that I am altogether subversive and shifty. On the whole, I live as honestly as possible, and the above was simply considering the hidden tensions of what motivates me. I think this may be true of you, too. I think what you do for us is incredible, but I do think also that this class has become a means to secure an alternative kind of power in your life, since the traditional route is out of the question. The institution may not recognize you with promotions; you may have somewhat less POWER amongst your peers, but you legitimately deserve a kind of stature, which you achieve by an alternative means: by shaping our college careers, and by winning special place in our hearts and minds.

I have often thought that the greatest character is shown not in achieving, but in being willing to sacrifice the prestige of achievement. I think you and I have both chosen the path of sacrificing public affirmation, but that old power thing is never gone for good. It works its way in my life insidiously, I don't even recognize it until...?

If you were teaching four classes (or however many a full-time prof teaches) even if you had no kids, there is NO WAY you would be able to give us the time and attention you do. If you had to wade through that many more papers, carry that many more conversations in your head, and all the bureaucracy that goes with that much more teaching, you would simply have to deal with us on a more superficial, generalized level. I value the specific attention you give me, and I think that you are able to do what your full-time counterparts can't possibly do, precisely because of the choices you have made.

This conversation reminds me of part of a message I heard recently at church. The pastor made the observation that sometimes humility becomes a source of pride. In the same way, sometimes sacrificing power becomes a source of power. (This is sort of similar to secondary gain, with the added benefit of being untouchable to criticism.)

Clearly laid out here are some of the reasons—pride and power—why we are not yet in paradise. This student's analysis of my motivation, particularly of the pride I take in my humility and marginality, seems to me quite accurate, troubling only because it marks so nakedly how much I love and need the work I do. But I want to lay alongside her claim its obverse, exploring here the possibility that my so-called marginality (which I now read, not so paradoxically, as privilege) might make me a better teacher, not only because I have more time to work with my students but because I am more vulnerable to them than are the tenured faculty, more aware of my dependence on and interdependence with them. (Certainly my re-appointments are contingent on their evaluations, year after year after year after year.)

In this exploration, I follow Maria Harris's suggestion that a vision of teaching that draws on the religious imagination can expand our sense of the work we do: "many of the problems of education are mysteries made shabby by the absence of reverence...we think in terms that are unworthy of us; we think too narrowly" (*Teaching* 25, 77). I draw heavily here on the wisdom of Christianity, which is so full of imaginative possibility for me as a teacher. Acutely aware of the presumptions and limitations of this kind of language, I employ it hoping that teachers who take offense at such imagery or cannot make use of it may feel invited thereby into other metaphoric possibilities.

Kenosis

Colleagues repeatedly remind me that the classroom is a place where only a certain very specific, very limited, kind of intellectual work is appropriate. (Church and therapy, they say, are available to facilitate other aspects of self-development.) Some years ago, for instance, when our staff of first-year writing teachers read together a chapter from Mary Rose O'Reilley's *The Peaceable Classroom,* a senior colleague dismissed the language of the text not as "salvational" but as "salivational." He objected that such language "made too much" of the students, evinced an inappropriate investment in who they might become. Similarly, our provost met my confession that I wanted my students to be "transformed in my presence" with the kind caution that "we ought to be more humble."

In response to such concerns, I look here at some of the possibilities of an ascetic teaching practice. I explore in particular the ways in which an adjunct position may facilitate such an approach, for much of my own teaching takes its impulse from my pronounced awareness of the tentative nature of my position on campus. Julia Kristeva suggests that such a sense of strangeness can open us to learning: "The ear is receptive to conflicts only if the body loses its footing. A certain imbalance is necessary, a swaying over some abyss" (17). Maria Harris draws similarly "on the experience of the *outsider*...as essential to any understanding of teaching" (*Teaching* xv). Henri Nouwen has also investigated the ways in which a sense of being marginal to the common enterprise might enable the kind of hospitality I try to practice in my classes:

> Once we have become poor, we can be a good host. It is...the paradox of hospitality...programs to prepare people for service...seldom train toward a voluntary poverty...But real training for service asks for a hard and often painful process of self-emptying...God did not reveal himself to us as the powerful other, unapproachable...Instead he came to us in Jesus Christ, who "emptied himself...and became as men are." (102–103, 106–108)

Nouwen focuses on the Christian understanding of *kenosis*, or emptying: Christ's relinquishing the form of God in becoming man and suffering death. Although part-time teaching involves the "emptying" of particular notions of academic achievement, in particular, the sacrifice of a certain amount of status and prestige, I can hardly claim that my regular, well-compensated, part-time employment qualifies as crucifixion. I do claim, however, that it may work quite well as ascetic practice.

The image of the academic as ascetic is well established but also misused and misunderstood. In *Exiles from Eden: Religion and the Academic Vocation in America*, Mark Schwehn uses Max Weber's famous 1918 address, "Wissenschaft als Beruf," as *locus classicus*

> for the predominant understanding of the academic calling...Weber's academics had to renounce...*in their callings*, spontaneous enjoyment, emotional satisfaction, and communal affections...modern academics gained a certain measure of alertness, intelligence, even freedom, by virtue of devotion to their callings, but they purchased them at enormous cost. (6, 14)

In 1939, Virginia Woolf asked newly educated Englishwomen whether they wished to join the "procession of educated men" and where that procession might lead them. Like Weber, she described a life of renunciation; even more than he, she emphasized the losses attendant on austere self-discipline and self-denial:

> if people are highly successful in their professions they lose their senses. Sight goes. They have no time to look at pictures. Sound goes. They have no time to listen to music. Speech goes. They have no time for conversation. They lose their sense of proportion—the relations between one thing and another. Humanity goes...And so competitive do they become that they will not share their work with others though they have more than they can do themselves. What then remains of a human being who has lost sight, sound, and sense of proportion? Only a cripple in a cave. (72)

Woolf's scenario has echoes as old as Plato's cave (to which I will return). It is also as contemporary as the *Philadelphia Inquirer,* which gives an account of the life of Virginia Lee, co-director of the Center for Neurodegenerative Disease Research at the University of Pennsylvania:

> Lee used to be a fabulous cook. No more. She loved music, thought she might be a professional pianist. No more. She used to enjoy being part of a knitting circle...Now there's no time. There's always another research paper to read, always another experiment to design, another student to guide. (D4)

Weber, Woolf and the *Inquirer* reporter, Shankar Vedantam, offer similar descriptions of the life of the professional researcher as an exercise in denial. Missing from all three is the sense of affirmation that motivates and rewards traditional Christian ascetic practice. As Schwehn observes, academics "have subjected themselves to this ascetic regimen without the religious consolations, assurances, and commitments that might have made sense of such self-abnegating behavior"; they "borrowed from a religious vocabulary whose meanings had been strangely inverted" (ix, 14).

The experience of teaching is similar: an act of "emptying" or giving of oneself that is paradoxically fulfilling. Similar, too, is the conventional Christian understanding of asceticism. In *Fullness of Life: Historical Foundations for a New Asceticism,* Margaret Miles describes the "specific psychological quality" of ascetic life as "joy" (46). The contributors to the massive volume (Wimbush and Valantasis 13) that records the International Conference on Asceticism, held at Union Theological Seminary in 1993, likewise depict "a state of plenitude rather than emptiness, a sense of presence rather than absence" (13). Geoff Harpham is perhaps the most astute of these in his insistence that, like all choices, the ascetic imperative involves "denial of something, gratification of something else": "Asceticism is a structure of compensation, in which something is granted—'treasure in heaven'—in return for something being given up—'all that thou hast'" ("Asceticism" 360).

I have come to a similar understanding of asceticism largely through my own spiritual tradition, which is a richly rewarding one. Our Quaker meetinghouse, like most, is spare and unadorned; there are no material or sensual aids to worship. The only cross takes some looking for: it is formed, faintly, by a few old, green-colored panes remaining in the windows. Missing, too, are the hymns of my Methodist childhood, the sermons and reading of scripture, all ritual and set practice, all that—for those of us who worship there—might distract from or interfere with the simple, unmediated experience of waiting in silence for God and speaking when we feel moved to do so.

I was first drawn to Quakerism by all this: by what it was not. I liked the way this sort of worship cast off rote, stripped away what I knew of conventional Christian exercise and routine, especially the minister and his sermon-on-how-I-should-live. It took me a while to learn just how and why this process of reduction, these gestures of withdrawal, facilitate my more profound immersion and engagement in the world. I slowly came to understand ascetic practice as a form of denial that, not at all paradoxically, is also an embrace: a disciplined attention to the world achieved only by continually disengaging ourselves from it. Barrett Brown cautioned Quakers in 1932 not to misunderstand this process: "It is easy to make a form of our very rejection of forms...It is a bold and colossal claim that we put forward—that the whole of life is sacramental" (90). Withdrawing from a busy life to worship together regularly in a silent, plain meetinghouse is a means of calling ourselves into a heightened awareness of the world around us.

Although this practice is, importantly, a communal form of meditation, it has some of the effects of private retirement. Henri Nouwen draws on the writings of Thomas Merton to explain how solitude

> makes real fellowship possible...: "It is in deep solitude that I find the gentleness with which I can truly love my brothers. The more solitary I am, the more affection I have for them"...Merton came to see...that solitude did not separate him from his contemporaries but instead brought him into a deep communion with them...The movement...to solitude ...is not a movement of a growing withdrawal from, but rather a movement toward, a deeper engagement in the burning issues of our time. (42, 61)

For Quakers like myself, the life of the householder—although not as stripped of the flesh as the monastic practice of Thomas Merton—may also fulfill an ascetic role. Miles writes of early Christian accounts of the "humility of attending to others" (142), even of marriage, with its "capacity to expose temptations to impatience, temper and self-seeking," as an ascetic discipline (161). My colleague Linda-Susan Beard, who is a monastic woman, has helped me understand how not only my worship time but the constant interruption of family life, the familiar routine of leaving work unfinished to attend to the needs of the family—even the unexpected call at the office to come care for a child who has taken sick at school—can function as ascetic practice. Her counsel has enabled me to respond to such needs as if to the ringing of a monastic bell, hearing each as sacrament: an invitation to listen beyond the narrowness of the task in which I am immediately engaged.

I was drawn to academics, as to Quakerism (long before I was drawn to Quakerism), because I learned so much from procedures of research and hard study. I found the attentive stripping away of what was extraneous, the disciplined focus of attention on a single line of inquiry, enormously clarifying. But stepping out of the physical labor, messy emotionalism, and financial uncertainties of my life and the lives of those who most concerned me into the methodical work of reading texts, their historical contexts, and their implications for the future has always been a temporary movement, always short lived. I frequently and regularly retreat from the intense engagement of scholarship to attend to other matters. I am an *ascetic* academic ascetic, periodically withdrawing from the life of withdrawal.

Because for so long I did not understand the congruence of these activities, the movement between my academic and other lives was often abrupt, and I experienced it as violent. Unable to leave scholarly work undone to attend to other needs, I dropped out of college and again out of graduate school when my studies came to seem too removed from more pressing concerns. And yet I always returned to academics, which functioned for me as a practice of withdrawal and reflection not unlike worship time, a sacrament that continually enabled me to re-engage the world, attentive to what was needed of-or-from me.

Life Emulsified

Academic work also early became for me an engagement with a community of scholars. I could not for long read alone but needed always to take that reading into conversation. The joy of our instructing one another, the talking back, the energizing practices of give and take have governed my more recent published work, and have always been central to my classrooms.

As conventional as the (inaccurate, inadequate) description of the academic researcher as ascetic is the opposition of such a life to and the privileging of such a life over the communal work of teaching. Schwehn begins his study of religion and the academic vocation "by unpacking one commonplace of academic life—the mysterious complaint, 'I don't have enough time to do my own work'":

> The fact that university faculty tend to think that classroom teaching and collegiality are strangely not part of their "own work" is a tribute to the socializing power of our graduate schools. There students learn…that research and publication constitute their tasks…[one conception] of the academic vocation…that of the academic as one who makes knowledge—has long since attained hegemony over all the others. (viii, 6)

In such a conception, the work of attending to the intellectual (ethical, moral, psychological) growth of undergraduates means turning one's attention from the exhilarating withdrawal of research and from the making of knowledge to which such research can lead to the weary task of forced re-immersion in the world, to the education of the young. Plato was perhaps the first—certainly he is among the most devastating—to describe what denial such practice involves. While Woolf described professional teachers as "cripples in a cave," Plato ascribed that image instead to those they instruct: each of those trained as philosophers must

> descend to where the rest of the community lives...[imprisoned] in a cavernous cell down under the ground...They've been there since childhood, with their legs and necks tied up in a way which keeps them in one place and allows them to look only straight ahead...[Glaucon protests that] we'll be wronging [the philosophers]: we'll be making the quality of their lives worse and denying them the better life they could be living... [But] the point of legislation is not to make one section of a community better off than the rest, but to engineer this for the community as a whole. (248, 240, 247, 248)

My conception of myself and of the work I do as a teacher differs considerably from Plato's plan for the philosophers. I see my ascetic practices, both religious and scholarly, not as self-denying descents into the cave which is the world, much less into classrooms of cripples situated within that world, but rather as disciplined means of enabling me to be more fully present both in the classroom and outside it.

According to Maria Lugones, such activity may also be profoundly undisciplining. Lugones uses the image of "curdling" to evoke her conception of a multiple selfhood which resists the ordering logic of purity, cannot be divided:

> the model of curdling...is a model for...border-dwellers, of people who live in a crossroads, people who deny purity...curdle-separation...is something we do in resistance to the logic of control, to the logic of purity...that we curdle testifies to our being active subjects, not consumed by the logic of control. Curdling...can become an art of resistance, metamorphosis, transformation. (477–478)

Lugones argues for a complex subjectivity that resists fragmentation. I share her refusal of division.

When I was a graduate student, I was taught that part-time work did not fit the operative academic paradigm. I was also offered the opportunity to help construct an alternative template. The invitation came from Maggie Mulqueen, herself then a graduate student in education. Maggie asked four departmental chairmen each to choose his "most competent" female graduate student and then conducted a series of separate, systematic interviews with the young women who were selected. I was one of those who described to Maggie a shared sense of our lives as complex juggling acts that moved constantly, ineptly, always a little off-kilter, to balance academic with familial interests.

On the basis of these interviews, Maggie wrote a dissertation, later a book, which articulated a sense of female competence derived not from achievement in a single arena but rather from balancing competing interests. She proposed

> a new theory, *balancing*...for promoting self-esteem...balancing emphasizes the important of *generalizing, diversifying,* and *integrating,* unlike [Robert White's standard description of competence] which focuses on specializing, narrowing, and selecting... Balancing is electing to apportion time...This model relies on a concept of competing equal priorities, thus focusing on integration rather than choice...the interactive essence of it necessitates continual, dynamic renegotiation. (16, 19, 175–176)

In the years since my life entered print in metaphoric balance, I have found myself increasingly dissatisfied with the limits of that image, particularly with the implication that its multiple aspects exist independently, in competition with others, and that I must continually renegotiate the appropriate amount of time I need to apportion to each. Reaching for a redefinition of the relationship between the academic, familial, communal, and spiritual aspects of my life, one more fully integrated than the dialectic of balance suggests, I have come to conceptualize and attempt to live my life in complex counterpoint: as an ascetic practice that calls me to be present and engaged in whatever I do, while never absent from the rest of it nor neglectful of its place within the whole.

Because academic life as I have theorized and lived it is not well described by the way Weber and Woolf use the term asceticism to invoke the practices of austere, costly self-denial, I'm proposing another image to evoke a different template: of an asceticism that fully embraces while as fully understanding the limits of the world in which my classes are situated.

One treat of working with colleagues in the sciences has been my introduction into whole new fields of metaphor. Kaye Edwards, who was trained as a developmental biologist, was searching for a term to describe the kind of life she and I were both seeking as mothers who were also teachers. Rejecting "balancing" as too rigid, too binary, and "juggling" as too tricky, too dangerous (who wants to think of her kids as a juggler's toys?), Kaye arrived at "emulsification": the suspension—not the mixing—of small globules of one liquid in a second. (Consider salad dressing, a mixture of oil and vinegar capable, with vigorous shaking, of being briefly combined but tending always to separate out.)

Using this image to conceptualize the relationship between my teaching and the rest of my life, I see myself as joyfully present to while-and-*because* detachedly absent from the classroom, aware always of a world of multiple dimensions that both informs and exceeds it. To "teach emulsified" is to keep the classroom in perspective, to have always a consciousness of the larger world in which it is suspended. Liable to stir things up in or to be stirred up by what happens beyond.

But liable, too, as Lugones says, to separate out:

> I am making mayonnaise...If I add too much oil at once, the mixture *se separa*, it separates...In English, one might say that the mayonnaise curdled. Mayonnaise is an oil-in-water emulsion. As all emulsions, it is unstable. When an emulsion curdles, the ingredients become separate from each other. But that is not altogether an accurate description: rather, they coalesce toward oil or toward water, most of the water becomes separate from most of the oil—it is instead, a matter of different degrees of coalescence. The same with mayonnaise; when it separates, you are left with yolky oil and oily yolk. (459)

It is to such "instability" that I now turn my attention.

Paradise Regained

From my experience as a Quaker, I have drawn an understanding of the ascetic imperative as a practice that structures oppositions, giving me the means to be detached from and responsive to the world at the same time. From my reading, I have gained a comprehension of scholarly practice as a "conspicuous instance of...this ascetic law of denial and compensation" (Harpham, "Asceticism" 359). From Maria Lugones, I have added an awareness of such separation as always incomplete, a curdling that leaves traces of the other while engaged in the same. I take now from Dante a figure who enacts such a process, a teacher who, like Plato's philosophers, descends from "a blissful place" to accompany her student but unlike them is moved by Love to do so (*Purgatory* II, l. 71).

The most profound, reverent, and enabling imagining I know of a teacher who is engaged yet detached, passionate yet ascetic, is that of Beatrice leading Dante through Paradise. As Sayers observes, she is "the heavenly schoolmistress who, having seen her pupil safely through his examination, goes on her way rejoicing. She looses him into freedom—even from herself—and he is willing to be set free" (*Purgatory* 36). For Dante, Beatrice is

> the earthly vessel in which the divine experience was carried...that experience of the Not-self—which, by arousing his adoring love, has become for him the God-bearing image, the revelation of the presence of God. Beatrice...represents his own personal experience of the immanence of the creator in the creature. (Sayers, *Hell* 68, *Paradise* 16)

And yet Beatrice neither falls in love nor entices Dante to do so again; rather, she works to wean him from that passion. "Beatrice shows no desire to possess Dante: she takes him with one hand only to give him away with the other" (Sayers, *Purgatory* 36). At the end of the poem, "no longer needed," Beatrice steps aside to let her student see for himself (Sayers, *Paradise* 331).

His journey, which so well enacts the restless desire which fuels much classroom work, returns us again to some of the dangers of the committed teaching life. Charles Williams demonstrated long ago the attentiveness to which Beatrice repeatedly calls Dante: "the general maxim of the whole way...is *attention*: 'look,' 'look well'" (16). But as recent interpretations of the *Commedia* make clear, Dante's description of what might happen under such careful tutelage is problematic for contemporary readers. Stephen Botterill, for instance, characterizes Beatrice's role as "the unquestioned source of authoritative doctrine" (121), and Teodolinda Bartolini attends to the "severely overdetermined" plot of the *Commedia,* the complacent certainty of the direction of its path (141–142). Robin Kirkpatrick has explored even more extensively the "disconcerting...possibility of perfection...leading to...impossible demands upon oneself and others" (104).

Kirkpatrick traces anew in the *Commedia* one of the lessons suggested by Toni Morrison's latest novel. A vision of paradise may well fuel righteous judgment: the desire to create a haven can lead to the exclusion, even the destruction, of those who can or will not conform to the ideal of perfection. Since I first began teaching, I have heard similar laments from my own students, who complain of my harsh demands, my excessive expectations for their achievement in my classes. At the close of a recent gender studies seminar, for instance, one student said that she felt

> pissed...that I was expected and pushed to voice an opinion on everything. The main thing I felt, *all the time,* was a real pressure to perform, to participate in some self-assured, overly opinionated way. This *forcing* to speak is not a way to help young feminists find their voices!

Such complaints have led me to a reconsideration of ascetic practices. I draw on asceticism now as resource and model for a form of teaching which, though less intrusive, is still expectant.

When I first read the *Commedia* in translation years ago, I was struck by a single passage of explication that continues to haunt me. In the notes to Canto IV of the Inferno, which describes the placement of the Virtuous Pagans in Limbo on the edge of the Pit of Hell, Dorothy Sayers explains, "the souls...enjoy that kind of after-life which they themselves imagined for the virtuous dead; *their failure lay in not imagining better.* They [fell short] in the imagination of ecstasy" (*Hell* 95, my emphasis).

It has been the task of my teaching career to examine the problematics of my classes, to name and interpret the difficulties that arise there, as prelude to imagining better. It has been the discovery of this chapter that "imagining better" may only exacerbate these difficulties: my students ofttimes experience my expectations as a heavy burden precisely because I bring into my classes years of preparation and as many years of accumulated hopes. In her teaching memoir, *Among the White Moon Faces*, Shirley Lim says similarly that many of her "community college students resented attention that demanded a reciprocal attentiveness" (214). Like Adam and Eve in the garden, they want to escape the expectant eye.

So now, as I teach, I try to remember the model of Beatrice, attempting with her to "simultaneously affirm and deny the value and importance" of the classroom work that we do, "being at once concerned with" and "wholly detached" from the texts, the students and the outcomes of our encounters (Sayers, *Paradise* 28). I take Beatrice as a model of ascetic practice, resource for a form of attentive teacherly engagement that is not intrusive, but still expectant.[1]

Attempting to teach as an ascetic, one whose full presence and engagement in the classroom is simultaneously an act of withdrawal, I find that Nouwen, again, articulates well what I intend:

> Someone who is filled with ideas, concepts, opinions and convictions cannot be a good host. There is no inner space to listen, no openness to discover the gift of the other...those "who know it all" can kill a conversation and prevent an interchange of ideas. Poverty of mind as a spiritual attitude is a growing willingness to recognize the incomprehensibility of the mystery of life...To prepare ourselves for service we have to prepare ourselves for an articulate not knowing...a learned ignorance...[with] less to say but much more to listen to. (103–105)

In describing a hospitable practice which offers "friendship without binding the guest" (71), which refrains from "burdening others with these divine expectations" (30), Nouwen offers a vision of community that, absent the Christian doctrine (well, the doctrine is not really subtractable), I like to imagine as a description of my classrooms:

> a waiting community, that is, a community which not only creates a sense of belonging but also a sense of estrangement. "We are together, but we cannot fulfill each other...we help each other, but we also have to remind each other that our destiny is beyond our togetherness." The support of the...community is a support in common expectation. Our eyes should not remain fixed on each other but be directed forward. The...community is not a closed circle of people embracing each other, but a forward-moving group of companions bound together by the same voice asking for their attention...[pilgrims] always moving forward. (153–154)

Such a conception of the classroom as a waiting community, not reliant on the teacher for completion, seeking fulfillment in some space beyond the one in which we gather, may address a number of the perceived problems of liberatory teaching as they have been articulated by my students and colleagues. A classroom of "pilgrims" may be particularly congenial for adjuncts like myself, whose on-campus marginality may tempt us to an inappropriate investment in the work that we do.

Reconceiving the college classroom as a space where the compensatory structure of the ascetic imperative might be enacted also speaks to the larger concern traced long ago by Weber and Woolf but executed ever more insistently today: our rather grim academic culture of professional discipline-as-denial. In reclaiming here the "celebratory practices and counterparts" of ascetic practice, I imagine the role that asceticism *could* play

> in the context of the oppressive—and life-denying—forces exemplified by powerful...professions...In this social context...ascetic withdrawal...can be done for the purpose of a more productive reengagement with society...[and might involve, for example] deliberate strategies for withdrawing from unhealthy patterns of work. Regimens of...ascetic behavior that seek to counter such controlling habits...can be understood as a form of political resistance. (Van Ness et al. *Asceticism* 591–593)

That may what I'm up to here, what this testimony is finally about and for.

 Openings

Talking, we leave the classroom.

I spoke in Meeting today of the mysterious slipping away of what I want to say in this book on teaching and learning. How hard it is to get it right.

> Adrienne Rich writes,
> *"We move   but our words stand*
> *Become responsible*
> *For more than we intended*
>
> *and this is verbal privilege"*
> ("North American Time" 325)

Speaking of her reluctance to publish, Sister Linda-Susan describes "the crucifixion of the text": having her words fixed on the page. While she moves on.

Why am I writing this book? To record my experiences of teaching, to try and understand them. I come to see the limits both of the recording and of the understanding.

> *"The process is dynamic. It has a mysterious element."* (Judy Logan, *Teaching Stories* 148)

Long ago, I went to Dorothy Steere with a question: how to teach my children the story of the resurrection? Her counsel: "just let them sit with the mystery."

My son Sam—fourteen now, moody, quiet, grumpy—is re-teaching me the same lesson. I ask him what is wrong, why he will not talk to me. He growls: "What is wrong? Why won't I talk to you? Why is the sky not purple?"

Cautioning me about intrusion, this young man reminds me not to push too hard to articulate what is not fully understood. What he has no desire to understand—even if understood, to speak. What is mystery.

Amid these accounts of openness, unstructuring, emptiness, silence, lie many counter-tales. Here's one.

It is spring 1982. About to finish graduate school at Penn, expecting my second child, I decide not to look for full-time work. My friends are not getting tenure, and I am afraid: afraid that, after six years of heavy work, I will not have a job and will have missed my children beginning their lives, what I am going into parenting for.

I tell a senior professor of my decision, ask his help in looking for part-time work. He says many things, but what I hear is—what still echoes years later—is this: "You are not marching with all your armies together." I am furious at what this seems to insinuate: that I am not in control of the pattern of my life. But I have carefully planned this pregnancy for the semester's end. Do I ask—or do I only think I do—"When is a woman supposed to have her children?"

"Hm...Romeo and Juliet might be good models."

Does he say that? Or do I just imagine the advice that young women like myself should have our children when we are very young—in order to get on with the "real" work of our lives, our academic careers, when we reach maturity?

I have told this story many times. Recording it now, I wonder how much of it is made up—imagination provoked by outrage, internal dialogue in which I write the script for others. Seventeen years later, I imagine seeking out this advisor, asking if the story sounds true to him. But what if I don't have it right?

I don't want him to take away this defining story. I still need it, scripted the way I have always told it.

The narrative, as I tell it, fits the parable I have shaped of my life, serves the explanation I have constructed to make sense of my location, as marginal/ outsider/part-timer in the academy.

> *Spivak's counsel, again: "one can make a strategy of taking away from [students] the authority of their marginality, the centrality of their marginality...that authority will not take them very far because the world is a large place. Others are many. The self is enclosed." (Outside in the Teaching Machine 18)*

I need this story as I have told and re-told it through the years, voicing the operative paradigm: "What is valued in the academy is full-time work, whatever the consequences to family life, to personal health and well-being."

> *"The stories we tell ourselves, particularly the silent or barely audible ones, are very powerful. They become invisible enclosures. Rooms with no air. One must open the window to see further, the door to possibility...How to tell a story without fashioning it along the prefabricated lines?...we are immersed in an old story and cannot see what is happening."* (Susan Griffin, *A Chorus of Stones* 284, 324)

Telling the story this way elides the complexities of my decision.

Yes, I was afraid to put myself on the market, afraid I would be tempted with an offer I would not be able to refuse. I chose to refuse the temptation. But I was also afraid that I would not be offered a job. Not putting myself to the test, I avoided failing it.

I begin to see why I tell the stories I do. What patterns they make, what functions they serve. How false they can be. How much they do not say.

Story:
1. The narrating or relating of an event or series of events, either true or fictitious.
4. An incident, experience, or subject that furnishes or would be interesting material for a narrative.
6. A report, a statement, or an allegation of facts.
8. An anecdote.
9. A lie.
10. Romantic legend or tradition.
From Latin, *historia*, from the Greek, *histor*, wisdom.
(*The American Heritage Dictionary of the English Language*)

> *"I wrote the story first. It was a true story. But it seemed too simple. So then I wrote the counter narrative: a second voice, second thoughts."* (Griffin, Reading at Bryn Mawr)

Story (2):
The set of rooms on the same level of a building. From Middle English storye, fr. Medieval latin *historia*, originally a row of windows with pictures on them, from Latin *historia*, story (tale). (*The American Heritage Dictionary*)

The house of fiction, Henry James told us, has many windows.

Telling my stories, I limit both the possibilities of my own life and the possibilities of others.

Towards the end of *Romeo and Juliet*, the prince of Verona counsels Montague, who is distraught at the death of his son:

> "Seal up the mouth of outrage for a while,
> Till we can clear these ambiguities,
> And know their spring, their head, their true descent;
> ...meantime forbear,

And let mischance be slave to patience." (V. iii. 216–221)

I know now that such ambiguities will never be cleared. But that is not what I was taught.

Another (not final) story. A junior at the College of William and Mary, in the spring of 1972, I take a course on Shakespearean tragedy. Professor Fehrenbach teaches us that only one of the plays, *King Lear*, is "really" tragic, because only there is the denouement inevitable. Only in *Lear* does character lead inexorably to ruin, revelation—and release. In all the other "tragedies"—in *Romeo and Juliet*, for instance—the sad endings are just near-misses, avoidable, escapable.

I love that analysis: such purity, such precision, such clarity and certainty. But that was thirty years ago. Teaching, drama, life have since come to seem much messier.

Returning now to the final lines of the play, I hear, still, the unsettledness of the conclusion. Not as tragic—Bob Fehrenbach was right about that—but as invitation to further talk, that interminable work we will never come to the end of:

> "A glooming peace this morning with it brings;
> The sun, for sorrow, will not show his head;
> Go hence, to have more talk of these sad things."
> (V. iii. 305–307)

Talking, still talking, we leave the classroom...

An ending that has no end...

With a laugh, Jeff supplies the epilogue: "Why 'tearning'? Why not 'leaching'?"

And so I begin again, with a new image: re-conceiving the class as a space for leaching, where what is solid dissolves. Porous, sieve-like, a place for percolating. A place for passing through.

Note

¹ In a July 2000 e-mail, Steve Smith wrote of a different way of conceptualizing this practice: "While Nietzeche's critique is brilliant and psychologically acute, he misreads true detachment (or, better, nonattachment) as cultivated in Buddhism, Hinduism and other such traditions. I think he is correct about the main strands of asceticism in the West (especially most monastic asceticism) as well as many strands in Asian thought; but there is a form of nonattachment, which I believe the Buddha had in mind, which does not involve denial but rather radical openness and receptivity—though without reactivity or expectation. Thus it does not generate the phenomenon of compensation. The classic image for this is the lotus flower, which is not removed from the muck but fully immersed in it, open and pristine while its roots dangle in muddy water.

The form of nonattachment I have in mind has many degrees and in its highest form (which might be likened in theistic imagery to residing in the mind of God) does not cling to any expected outcome and has no needs regarding, say, students' responses to one's teaching efforts. One gives out of plenitude and does not expect or need reciprocity or compensation, since one is already full.

Though only a few saints, arhats, buddhas and the like may have achieved such a state, everyone occupies a place on this continuum, and may move on that continuum by virtue of spiritual practice and grace. So—it is possible to reduce one's level of expectations and needs and become more content with just doing what one does, because that is what one does."

Bibliography

Allison, Dorothy. "Femme." *Skin: Talking About Sex, Class and Literature.* Ithaca, New York: Firebrand Books, 1994. 151–158.

The American Heritage Dictionary of the English Language. New College Edition. Ed. William Morris. Boston Houghton Mifflin, 1979.

Anderson, Penelope. Newsgroup Entry. General Programs 290. Bryn Mawr College. Spring 1998.

Annas, Pamela. "radicalteacher definition." *Politics of Education: Essays from "Radical Teacher."* Ed. Susan O'Malley, et al. Albany: State University of New York, 1990. 339–340.

Arendt, Hannah. "Philosophy and Politics." *Social Research* 57, 1 (Spring 1990): 73–103.

Bacon, Margaret Hope. *Mothers of Feminism: The Story of Quaker Women in America.* San Francisco: Harper and Row, 1986.

Baer-Schimmel, Roberta. Note with a late paper. Liberal Studies 2. Bryn Mawr College. Spring 1996.

Baker, Houston Jr. *Long Black Song: Essays on Black American Literature and Culture.* Charlottesville: University Press of Virginia, 1972.

Barnes, Kathy. "Talking Like a Man, Going Ape, and Bryn Mawr: Finishing College at Forty-Eight." Senior Seminar Paper. Bryn Mawr College. May 1, 1998.

Bartolini, Teodolinda, and Mowbray Allan. "Critical Exchange." *MLN* 105, 1 (1990): 138–149.

Bauman, Richard. *Let Your Words Be Few: Symbolism of Speaking and Silence Among Seventeenth-Century Quakers.* New York: Cambridge, 1993.

Belenky, Mary Field, et al. "Connected Teaching." *Women's Ways of Knowing.* New York: Basic, 1986. 214–229.

Berthoff, Ann. "Interchanges: Spiritual Sites of Composing." *CCC* 45, 2 (May 1994): 237–262.

Bickford, Susan. *Dissonance of Democracy: Listening, Conflict and Citizenship.* Ithaca, New York: Cornell University Press, 1996.

Bopp, Jennifer. "The End of Mawrtyrdom." Liberal Studies 2. Bryn Mawr College. Spring 1997.

Bordo, Susan. "Feminism, Postmodernism, and Gender Scepticism." *Feminism/Postmodernism*, ed. Linda Nicholson. New York: Routledge, 1990. 133–156.

Botterill, Steven. "Life After Beatrice: Bernard of Clairvaux in Paradiso XXXI." *Texas Studies in Language and Literature* 32, 1 (Spring 1990): 120–136.

Bourdieu, Pierre, and Jean-Claude Passeron. *Reproduction in Education, Society and Culture.* Trans. Richard Nice. 1977; rpt. New York: Sage, 1990.

Bracci, Linda. "Undefining Sex with the Female Orgasm." General Programs 252. Women, Medicine and Biology. Haverford College. Fall 1997.

Bracket, Joseph. "Simple Gifts." American Shaker Tune. *Songs of the Spirit.* Philadelphia: Religious Education Committee of Friends General Conference, 1978.

Braidotti, Rosi. "Beyond Deconstruction: Debates Between Feminist Post-Colonials and Poststructuralism." Penn Mid-Atlantic Seminar for the Study of Women and Society. The University of Pennsylvania. December 5, 1995.

Brown, Barrett. 1932; rpt. Philadelphia Yearly Meeting of the Religious Society of Friends. *Faith and Practice: A Book of Christian Discipline.* 1955; rev. Philadelphia: Philadelphia Yearly Meeting, 1997.

Brunner, Diane D. *Inquiry and Reflection: Framing Narrative Practice in Education.* Albany: State University of New York Press, 1994.

Bryn Mawr: The Undergraduate College Catalog and Calendar 2000–2001.

Butler, Judith. "Imitation and Gender Subordination." *Inside/Out: Lesbian Theories, Gay Theories,* ed. Diana Fuss. New York: Routledge, 1989.

———. "Gender is Burning." *Bodies That Matter.* New York: Routledge, 1993. 121–140.

———. *Excitable Speech: A Politics of the Performative.* New York: Routledge, 1997.

Bynum, Caroline. "Why All the Fuss about the Body? A Medievalist's Perspective." *Critical Inquiry* 22, 1 (Autumn 1995): 1–33.

Campbell, Sarah. "Emergen/t/c/y." November 1994.

———. "The Voice of the Turtle." English 016. Bryn Mawr College. Spring 1995.

Chicago, Judy. *The Dinner Party: A Symbol of Our Heritage.* Garden City, New Jersey: Anchor/Doubleday, 1979.

Coffin, William Sloane. "The Good News About the Brokenhearted Christian Blues." *U.S. Catholic* 51 (August 1986): 28–30.

Conner, Alisa. "Feminist Pedagogy and the Feminist and Gender Studies Program at Bryn Mawr College: Reading the Stories." Senior Thesis. Bryn Mawr College. April 1994.

Corrigan, Philip. *Social Forms/Human Capacities: Essays in Authority and Difference.* London: Routledge, 1990.

Culley, Margo, and Catherine Portuges, eds. *Gendered Subiects: The Dynamics of Feminist Teaching.* Boston: Routledge and Kegan Paul, 1985.

Culley, Margo. "Anger and Authority in the Introductory Women's Studies Classroom." *Gendered Subjects: The Dynamics of Feminist Teaching.* 209–217.

Dante Alighieri. *The Comedy.* Trans. Dorothy Sayers. Harmondsworth, Middlesex: Penguin, 1950–1962.

De Beauvoir, Simone. *The Second Sex.* 1949; rpt. and trans. H.M. Parshley. New York: Vintage, 1974.

Dent, Gina. "Missionary Position." *To Be Real: Telling the Truth and Changing the Face of Feminism.* New York: Anchor, 1995. 61–75.

Diamond, Elin. "The Shudder of Catharsis in Twentieth-Century Performance." *Performativity and Performance*, ed. Parker and Sedgwick. 152–172..

Downing, Michael. *Perfect Agreement.* New York: Berkley Books, 1997.

Duchovnay, Minna Canton. "The Pedagogy of the Spider." English 016. Bryn Mawr College. Spring 1994.

Dunn, Kathleen. "Feminist Teaching: Who Are Your Students?" *Women's Studies Quarterly* 15, 34 (Fall-Winter 1987): 40–46.

Duras, Marguerite. *The Lover.* Trans. Barbara Bray. New York: Harper and Row, 1985.

Elbow, Peter. "The Pedagogy of the Bamboozled." *Embracing Contraries.* New York: Oxford, 1986. 87–98.

Ellsworth, Elizabeth. "Why Doesn't This Feel Empowering? Working Through the Repressive Myths of Critical Pedagogy." *Feminisms and Critical Pedagogy,* ed. Luke and Gore. 90–119.

Felman, Shoshana. "Psychoanalysis and Education." *Learning Desire: Perspectives on Pedagogy, Culture and the Unsaid.* Ed. Sharon Todd. New York: Routledge, 1997.

Fine, Michelle. "Sexuality, Schooling, and Adolescent Females: The Missing Discourse Of Desire." *Disruptive Voices: The Possibility of Feminist Research.* Ann Arbor: University of Michigan, 1992. 31–60.

Finke, Laurie. "Knowledge as Bait: Feminism, Voice, and the Pedagogical Unconscious." *College English* 55, 1 (January 1993). 7–27.

Fish, Stanley. "The Common Touch, or, One Size Fits All." *The Politics of Liberal Education.* Ed. Darryl J. Gless and Barbara Herrnstein Smith. Durham : Duke University Press, 1992. 241–266.

Fiumara, Gemma Corradi. *The Other Side of Language: A Philosophy of Listening.* New York: Routledge, 1990.

Foucault, Michel. *The History of Sexuality.* Trans. Robert Hurley. New York: Pantheon, 1978.

Fox, George. The Journal and the Epistles. Rpt. *Quaker Spirituality: Selected Writings.* Ed. Douglas Steere. New York: Paulist, 1984. 57–136.

Freire, Paulo. *Pedagogy of the Oppressed.* Trans. Myra Berman Ramos. New York: Continuum, 1990.

———. "The Catholic University: Reflections on its Task." Villanova University. November 20, 1991.

Friends Association for Higher Education. Thirteenth Annual Conference. Bryn Mawr College. Bryn Mawr, Pennsylvania. June 19–23, 1992.

Gallop, Jane, ed. *Pedagogy: The Question of Impersonation.* Bloomington: Indiana University Press, 1995.

Gappa, Judith, and David Leslie. *The Invisible Faculty: Improving the Status of Part-Timers in Higher Education*. San Francisco: Jossey-Bass, 1993.

Geertz, Clifford. "Thick Description: Toward an Interpretive Theory of Culture." *The Interpretation of Cultures: Selected Essays*. New York: Basic, 1973. 3–30.

Gordon, Mary. *Spending: A Utopian Divertimento*. New York: Scribner, 1998.

Gore, Jennifer. "What We Can Do For You! What Can 'We' Do For 'You'? Struggling over Empowerment in Critical and Feminist Pedagogy." *Feminisms and Critical Pedagogy*, ed. Luke and Gore. 54–73.

———. *The Struggle for Pedagogies: Critical and Feminist Discourses as Regimes of Truth*. New York: Routledge, 1993.

Griffin, Susan. *A Chorus of Stones: The Private Life of War*. New York: Anchor, 1992.

———. Reading at Bryn Mawr College. February 2, 1999.

Harpham, Geoffrey Galt. *The Ascetic Imperative in Culture and Criticism*. Chicago: The University of Chicago Press, 1987.

———. "Asceticism and the Compensations of Art." *Asceticism*, ed. Vincent Wimbush and Richard Valantasis. 357–368.

Harris, Maria. *Women and Teaching: Themes for a Spirituality of Pedagogy*. Mahwah, New Jersey: Paulist, 1988.

———. *Teaching and the Religious Imagination: An Essay in the Theology of Teaching*. San Francisco: Harper, 1991.

Hedges, Elaine, and Shelley Fisher Fishkin, eds. *Listening to the Silences: New Essays in Feminist Criticism*. New York: Oxford, 1994.

Hedley, Jane, and JoEllen Parker. "Writing Across the Curriculum: The Vantage of the Liberal Arts." *ADE Bulletin*, 98 (Spring 1991): 22–28.

Hoagland, Sarah. "Some Thoughts About 'Caring.'" *Feminist Ethics*, ed. Claudia Card. Lawrence: University Press of Kansas, 1991. 246–263.

Hole, Helen. *Things Civil and Useful: A Personal View of Quaker Education*. Richmond, Indiana: Friends United Press, 1978.

hooks, bell. *Teaching to Transgress: Education as the Practice of Freedom*. New York: Routledge, 1994.

Horowitz, Helen. *Alma Mater: Design and Experience in the Women's Colleges from Their Nineteenth-Century Beginnings to the 1930s.* New York: Knopf, 1984.

Hubbard, Geoffrey. *Quaker by Convincement.* 1974; rpt. London: Penguin, 1985.

Hulbert, Ann. Review of *The Kindness of Children,* by Vivian Paley. *New York Times Book Review.* April 4, 1999: 23.

Irigaray, Luce. "How to Define Sexuate Rights?" Trans. David Macey. *The Irigaray Reader.* Ed. Margaret Whitford. Cambridge, Massachusetts: Basil Blackwell, 1991. 204–212.

———. "Belief Itself" (1980), "Divine Women" (1984), and "The Three Genders" (1986). *Sexes and Geneologies.* Trans. Gillian Gill. New York: Columbia University Press, 1993. 23–53, 55–72, 167–184.

———. "Love of the Other." *An Ethics of Sexual Difference.* Trans. Carolyn Burke and Gillian Gill. Ithaca: Cornell University Press, 1993. 133–150.

Jaggers, Alison. *Feminist Politics and Human Nature.* Totowa, New Jersey: Rowman and Allanheld, 1983.

Jay, Martin. "In the Empire of the Gaze: Foucault and the Denigration of Vision in Twentieth-century French Thought." *Foucault: A Critical Reader.* Ed. David Couzens Hoy. New York: Basil Blackwell, 1986. 175–204.

Johnson, Barbara. *The Feminist Difference: Literature, Psychoanalysis, Race, and Gender.* Cambridge: Harvard University Press, 1998.

Jones, Amelia. "Sexual Politics: Feminist Strategies, Feminist Conflicts, Feminist Histories." *Sexual Politics: Judy Chicago's The Dinner Party in Feminist Art History.* University of California Press, 1996. 20–45.

———. "The 'Sexual Politics' of *The Dinner Party*: A Critical Context." *Sexual Politics,* ed. Amelia Jones. 82–125.

Jones, Bill T. and Bill Moyers. *Still/Here.* Videocassette. David Grubin Productions and Public Affairs Television, 1997.

Joselit, David. "Identity Politics: Exhibiting Gender." *Art in America* 85, 1 (January 1997). 36–39.

Kaplan, Carla. *The Erotics of Talk: Women's Writing and Feminist Paradigms.* New York: Oxford, 1996.

Kauffman, Hilda. "What is in the Attic of this Classroom?" English 015. Bryn Mawr College. Fall 1993.

Kauffman, Linda. "The Long Goodbye: Against Personal Testimony, or An Infant Grifter Grows Up." *Feminisms: An Anthology of Literary Theory and Criticism.* Ed. Robyn Warhol and Diane Price Herndl. New Brunswick, New Jersey: Rutgers University Press, 1997. 1155–1171.

Kelly, Ursula. *Schooling Desire: Literacy, Cultural Politics, and Pedagogy.* New York: Routledge, 1997.

Kirkpatrick, Robin. "Dante's Beatrice and the Politics of Singularity." *Texas Studies in Literature and Language* 32, 1 (Spring 1990): 101–119.

Kocsis, Deborah. "Warm Fuzzies," "Cold Pricklies," and Turtles. English 016. Bryn Mawr College. Spring 1995.

Koehn, Daryl. *Rethinking Feminist Ethics: Care, Trust and Empathy.* New York: Routledge, 1998.

Koestenbaum, Wayne. *Double Talk: The Erotics of Male Literary Collaboration.* New York: Routledge, 1989.

Kristeva, Julia. *Strangers to Ourselves.* Trans. Leon Roudiez. New York: Columbia, 1991.

Lacey, Paul. *Education and the Inward Teacher.* Pendle Hill Pamphlet 278. Wallingford, Pennsylvania: Pendle Hill Publications, 1988.

———. "Inviting the Inward Teacher." Lecture. Pendle Hill. Wallingford, Pennsylvania. November 5, 1990.

Lakoff, George, and Mark Johnson. *Metaphors We Live By.* Chicago: University of Chicago Press, 1980.

Lather, Patti. *Getting Smart: Feminist Research and Pedagogy With/In the Postmodern.* New York: Routledge, 1991.

Lauter, Paul, ed. *Reconstructing American Literature: Courses, Syllabi, Issues.* Old Westbury, New York: The Feminist Press, 1983.

Leatherman, Courtney. "Do Accreditors Look the Other Way When Colleges Rely on Part-Timers?" *Chronicle of Higher Education* 44, 11 (November 7, 1997): A12–A14.

———. "Faculty Unions Move to Organize Growing Ranks of Part-Time Professors." *Chronicle of Higher Education* 44, 25 (February 27, 1998): A12–A14.

Leiva, Claudia. "Straight Line-Anne, Zig-Zag Claudia." English 016. Bryn Mawr College. Spring 1995.

Lewis, Magda, and Roger Simon. "A Discourse Not Intended for Her: Learning and Teaching Within Patriarchy." *Harvard Educational Review* 56, 4 (November 1986). 457–472.

Lewis, Magda Gere. *Without A Word: Teaching Beyond Women's Silence.* New York: Routledge, 1993.

Lim, Shirley Geok-lin. *Among the White Moon Faces: An Asian-American Memoir of Homelands.* New York: The Feminist Press, 1996.

Litterine, Lynn. Journal. English 280. Bryn Mawr College. Spring 1994.

Logan, Judy. *Teaching Stories.* New York: Kodansha International, 1997.

López, Belkys. "Turtle Storm." Liberal Studies 2. Bryn Mawr College. Spring 1997.

Lorde, Audre. "For Each of You." 1970; rpt. *Chosen Poems, Old and New.* New York: Norton, 1982.

Lugones, Maria. "Purity, Impurity, and Separation." *Signs* 19, 2 (Winter 1994): 458–477.

Luke, Carmen, and Jennifer Gore, eds. *Feminisms and Critical Pedagogy.* New York: Routledge, 1992.

Luttrell, Wendy. "'The Teachers, They All Had Their Pets': Concepts of Gender, Knowledge, and Power." *Signs* 18, 3 (1993): 505–546.

Maher, Frances. "Classroom Pedagogy and the New Scholarship on Women." *Gendered Subjects,* ed. Culley and Portuges. 29–48.

McCloskey, Donald V. "Storytelling in Economics." *Narrative in Culture: The Uses of Storytelling in the Sciences, Philosophy and Literature.* Ed. Cristopher Nash. New York: Routledge, 1990.

McFague, Sally. *The Body of God: An Ecological Theology.* Minneapolis: Fortress, 1973.

McIntosh, Peggy. "Interactive Phases of Curricular Re-Vision: A Feminist Perspective." Working Paper No. 124. Wellesley College Center for Research on Women. 1983.

Meyer, Laura. "From Finish Fetish to Feminism: Judy Chicago's *Dinner Party* in California Art History." *Sexual Politics,* ed. Amelia Jones. 46–81.

Miles, Margaret. *Fullness of Life: Historical Foundations for a New Asceticism.* Philadelphia: Westminster Press, 1981.

Miller, Andrea. E-mail. Liberal Studies 2. Bryn Mawr College. Fall 1996.

Moschkovich, Judit. " —But I Know You, American Woman." *This Bridge Called My Back: Writing by Radical Women of Color.* Ed. Cherrie Moraga and Gloria Anzaldua. New York: Kitchen Table/Women of Color Press, 1983. 79–84.

Moon, Amanda. E-mail. General Programs 290. Bryn Mawr College. Spring 1998.

Moore, Marianne. "Silence." *The Complete Poems.* 1967; rpt. New York: Penguin, 1982.

Morrison, Toni. *Paradise.* New York: Knopf, 1998.

Mulqueen, Maggie. *On Our Own Terms: Redefining Competence and Femininity.* Albany: State University of New York Press, 1992.

Newman, Kim. Letter. June 3, 1998.

Noddings, Nel. *The Challenge to Care in Schools: An Alternative Approach to Education.* New York: Teachers' College Press, 1992.

Nouwen, Henri. *Reaching Out: The Three Movements of the Spiritual Life.* Garden City, New York: Doubleday, 1986.

O'Donnell, Sheryl. "Teaching/(M)othering: The Feminist Classroom as Unbounded Text." *Narrating Mothers: Theorizing Maternal Subjectivities.* Ed. Brenda O. Daly and Maureen T. Reddy. Knoxville: The University of Tennessee Press, 1991. 258–273.

Olmstead, Sterling. "Motion of Love: A John Woolman Retreat." Pendle Hill. Wallingford, Pennsylvania. June 3–5, 1994.

O'Reilley, Mary Rose. "The Inwardly Mobile: Education in the Opposite Direction." Lecture. Pendle Hill. Wallingford, Pennsylvania. October 22, 1990.

———. *The Peaceable Classroom.* Portsmouth, New Hampshire: Boynton/Cook, 1993.

———. *Radical Presence: Teaching as Contemplative Activity.* Portsmouth, New Hampshire: Boynton/Cook, 1998.

Orner, Mimi. "Interrupting the Calls for Student Voice in 'Liberatory' Education: A Feminist Poststructuralist

Perspective." *Feminisms and Critical Pedagogy*, ed. Luke and Gore. 74–89.

Owens, Craig. *Beyond Recognition: Representation, Power, and Culture.* Ed. Scott Bryson, Barbara Kruger, Lynne Tillman and Jane Weinstock. Berkeley: University of California Press, 1992.

Palmer, Parker. "Meeting for Learning: Education in a Quaker Context." *The Pendle Hill Bulletin* 284 (May 1976).

———. *To Know as We Are Known: Education as a Spiritual Journey.* 1983; rpt. San Francisco: Harper, 1993.

———. *The Courage to Teach: Exploring the Inner Landscape of a Teacher's Life.* San Francisco: Jossey-Bass, 1998.

Parker, Andrew, and Eve Kosofsky Sedgwick, eds. *Performativity and Performance.* New York: Routledge, 1995.

Penington, Isaac. Letter LII. *Letters.* Ed. John Barclay. London: John and Arthur Arch, 1637; rpt. 1828.

Penn,William. *Advice of William Penn to his Children, Relating to Their Civil and Religious Conduct.* 1726; rpt. Philadelphia: F. Roberts, 1881. Chapter II, Section 27.

Phillips, Mary Lou. "A Ministry of Attention and Touch." *Friends Journal* 46, 4 (April 2000): 6–9.

Pinar, William and Madeline Grumet. *Toward a Poor Curriculum.* Dubuque, Iowa: Kendall/Hunt, 1976.

Plato. *Republic.* Trans. Robin Waterfield. New York: Oxford University Press, 1993.

Potok, Chaim. *The Chosen.* New York: Simon and Schuster, 1967.

Raymond, Janice. "Women's Studies: A Knowledge of One's Own." *Gendered Subiects*, ed. Culley and Portuges. 49–63.

Reichel, Myra. "Pedagogy of the Would-Be Student." English 016. Bryn Mawr College Spring 1992.

———. "works in progress." English 016. Bryn Mawr College. Spring 1992.

Revel, Jean-Francoise, and Matthieu Ricard. *The Monk and the Philosopher.* New York: Schocken, 1999.

Rich, Adrienne. "Cartographies of Silence." *The Dream of a Common Language: Poems 1974–1977.* New York: Norton, 1978.

———. "North American Time." *Your Native Land, Your Life: Poems.* New York: Norton, 1986.

Ricoeur, Paul. *The Rule of Metaphor: Multidisciplinary Studies of the Creation of Meaning in Language.* Trans. Robert Czerny. Toronto: University of Toronto, 1975.

Rosaldo, Renato. *Culture and Truth: The Remaking of Social Analysis.* Boston: Beacon, 1993.

Salomon, Jeanne-Rachel. Notes. Liberal Studies 2. Bryn Mawr College. Fall 1996, Spring 1997.

———. "Pedagogy of the Stuffed Goose." Liberal Studies 2. Bryn Mawr College. Spring 1997.

Schell, Eileen. *Gypsy Academics and Mother-Teachers: Gender, Contingent Labor, and Writing Instruction.* Portsmouth, New Hampshire: Boynton/Cook, 1998.

Schmucker, Nancy. "Listening: The Lesson at the Big Table in the Center of the Porch." English 016. Bryn Mawr College. Spring 1994.

Schutz, Aaron, and Anne Ruggles Gere. "Service Learning and English Studies: Rethinking 'Public Service.'" *College English* 160, 2 (February 1998): 29–149.

Schwehn, Mark. *Exiles from Eden: Religion and the Academic Vocation in America.* New York: Oxford, 1993.

Scott, Joan. "'Experience.'" *Feminists Theorize the Political*, ed. Judith Butler and Joan Scott. New York: Routledge, 1992. 22–40.

Scott, Patricia. "Reflections." English 016. Bryn Mawr College. Spring 1995.

Shakespeare, William. *Romeo and Juliet. The Complete Works.* Ed. Hardin Craig. Glenview, Illinois: Scott, Foresman, 1961.

Sheeran, Michael. *Beyond Majority Rule: Voteless Decisions in the Religious Society of Friends.* Philadelphia: Philadelphia Yearly Meeting, 1983.

Simon, Roger. *Teaching Against the Grain: Tests for a Pedagogy of Possibility.* New York: Bergin and Garvey, 1992.

Sollors, Werner. *Beyond Ethnicity: Consent and Descent in American Culture.* New York: Oxford University, 1986.

Sontag, Susan. "The Aesthetics of Silence." *Styles of Radical Will.* New York: Farrar, Straus and Giroux, 1969. 3–34.

———. *AIDs and Its Metaphors.* New York: Farrar, Straus, and Giroux, 1989.

Spivak, Gayatri. "Can the Subaltern Speak?" *Marxism and the Interpretation of Culture.* Ed. Gary Nelson and Lawrence Grossberg. Urbana: University of Illinois, 1988. 271-313.

———. *Outside in the Teaching Machine.* New York: Routledge, 1993.

Stanton, Ann. "Reconfiguring Teaching and Knowing in the College Classroom." *Knowledge, Difference, and Power: Essays Inspired by Women's Ways of Knowing.* Ed. Nancy Goldberger, Jill Tarule, Blythe Clinchy, and Mary Belenky. New York: Basic, 1996. 25–56.

Stein, Gertrude. *Geography and Plays.* 1922; rpt. New York: Something Else Press, 1968.

Stephens, Caroline. "Quaker Strongholds." 1890; rpt. *Quaker Spirituality: Selected Writings.* Ed. Douglas Steere. New York: Paulist, 1984. 239–258.

Stockton, Kathryn Bond. *God Between Their Lips: Desire Between Women in Irigaray, Bronte and Eliot.* Stanford: Stanford University Press, 1994.

Sugg, Redding, Jr. *Motherteacher: The Feminization of America Education.* Charlottesville: University Press of Virginia, 1978.

Taylor, Ernest. *Richard Hubberthorne: Soldier and Preacher.* Friends Ancient and Modern, #16. New York: Friends' Tract Association, 1911.

Todd, Sharon, ed. *Learning Desire: Perspectives on Pedagogy, Culture and the Unsaid.* New York: Routledge, 1997.

Tompkins, Jane. "Pedagogy of the Distressed." *College English* 52, 6 (1990): 653–660.

———. *A Life in School: What the Teacher Learned.* Reading, Massachusetts: Addison-Wesley, 1996.

Tracy, David. "Metaphor and Religion: The Test Case of Christian Texts." *On Metaphor.* Ed. Sheldon Sacks. Chicago: University of Chicago, 1979. 89–104.

Tran, Djung. Newsgroup Entry. General Programs 290. Bryn Mawr College. Spring 1998.

Van Ness, Peter, with Richard Valantasis, Paul Julian, Gillian Lindt, Elaine Pagels, Ehsan Yarshater. "Practices and Meanings of Asceticism in Contemporary Religious Life and

Culture: A Panel Discussion." *Asceticism*, ed. Vincent Wimbush and Richard Valantasis. 588–606.

Vedantam, Shankar. "Devoted to each other and Alzheimer's work." *Philadelphia Inquirer* (Oct. 19, 1998): D1, D4.

Visweswaran, Kamala. *Fictions of Feminist Ethnography.* Minneapolis: University of Minnesota, 1994.

Walzer, Michael. *Interpretation and Social Criticism.* Cambridge: Harvard University Press, 1987.

Weil, Simone. "Reflections on the Right Use of School Studies with a View to the Love of God." *Waiting for God.* Trans. Emma Craufurd. 1951; rpt. New York: Harper and Row, 1973. 105–116.

Weiler, Kathleen. "Freire and a Feminist Pedagogy of Difference." *Harvard Education Review* 61, 4 (November 1991): 449–470.

Welch, Sharon. *A Feminist Ethic of Risk.* Minneapolis: Fortress, 1990.

Wendell, Susan. *The Rejected Body: Feminist Philosophical Reflections on Disability.* New York: Routledge, 1996.

Williams, Charles. *The Figure of Beatrice: A Study in Dante.* London: Faber and Faber, 1943.

Willis, Emily. "*We* tell the Stories." Liberal Studies 2. Bryn Mawr College. Spring 1997.

Wilson, Robin. "For Some Adjunct Faculty Members, the Tenure Track Holds Little Appeal." *Chronicle of Higher Education* 44, 46 (July 24, 1998): A8–A9.

Wimbush, Vincent and Richard Valantasis, eds. *Asceticism.* New York: Oxford University Press, 1995.

Woolf, Virginia. *Three Guineas.* 1939; rpt. New York: Harcourt Brace, 1966.

Woolman, John. *The Journal and Major Essays.* Ed. Phillips P. Moulton. Richmond, Indiana: Friends United Press, 1989.

Worthen, W. B. "Drama, Performativity, and Performance." *PMLA* 113, 5 (October 1998): 1093–1107.

Yeats, William Butler. "The Second Coming." 1921; rpt. *The Collected Poems.* New York: Macmillan, 1977.

Yeazell, Ruth. *Language and Knowledge in the Late Novels of Henry James.* Chicago: University of Chicago Press, 1976.

Young, Iris Marion. "The Ideal of Community and the Politics of Difference." *Feminism/Postmodernism.* Ed. Linda Nicholson. New York: Routledge, 1990. 300–323.

Index

STUDIES IN

Peter L. Laurence &
Victor H. Kazanjian, Jr.
General Editors

EDUCATION & SPIRITUALITY

Studies in Education and Spirituality presents the reader with the most recent thinking about the role of religion and spirituality in higher education.
It includes a wide variety of perspectives, including students, faculty, administrators, religious life and student life professionals, and representatives of related educational and religious institutions. These are people who
have thought deeply about the topic and share their insights and experiences through this series. These works address the questions: What is the
impact of religious diversity on higher education? What is the potential of
religious pluralism as a strategy to address the dramatic growth of religious
diversity in American colleges and universities? To what extent do institutions of higher learning desire to prepare their students for life and work in
a religiously pluralistic world? What is the role of spirituality at colleges and
universities,
particularly in relationship to teaching and learning pedagogy, the
cultivation of values, moral and ethical development, and the fostering of
global learning communities and responsible global citizens?

For additional information about this series or for the submission of manu-
scripts, please contact:

    Peter L. Laurence
    5 Trading Post Lane
    Putnam Valley, NY 10579

To order other books in this series, please contact our Customer Service
Department:

    (800) 770-LANG (within the U.S.)
    (212) 647-7706 (outside the U.S.)
    (212) 647-7707 FAX

Or browse online by series:

    www.peterlangusa.com